PERSIAN CATS

PERSIAN CATS

GRACE POND F.Z.S.

Revised edition

FOYLES HANDBOOKS
LONDON

ISBN 0 7071 0632 X

© W. & G. Foyle Ltd. 1964

Reprinted 1972
Reprinted 1975
Revised edition 1980

The photographs in this book were taken by Mrs. A. Cumbers.

Published in Great Britain by
W. & G. Foyles Ltd.,
125 Charing Cross Road,
London WC2H 0EB

Photoset and printed by
Photobooks (Bristol) Ltd.

CONTENTS

ILLUSTRATIONS

1

A SHORT HISTORY OF PERSIAN CATS

THE ORIGIN of the Persian or long-haired cat is a subject of much conjecture. At one time it was thought that the European Wild Cat, still found in parts of Europe, and its Scottish equivalent was the ancestor of our Persian pedigree varieties. This theory has now been rejected as their characteristics differ considerably, although the wild cat is known to interbreed, given the opportunity, with local cats. On the whole it is a coarser, heavier-built animal, with squarer head and higher legs. The tail is shorter, bushier, with equal thickness throughout. The coat is very thick, but its length cannot compare with the coat of a pedigree specimen. Another theory also now discarded was that a fearsome-looking, but beautifully marked and wonderfully-coloured member of the feline family known as Pallas's cat, found in Tibet and Mongolia, was the ancestor responsible for the long coat. I imagine the first long hairs occurred by chance, a mutation, and because of the attractive appearance, the cats were cared for and the kittens possibly cherished, thus establishing a strain with long fur.

Practically every cat book written mentions the fact that the known history of the domestic cat dates from the time of the Ancient Egyptians, but, however much research one does, there seems to be no mention of cats with long coats in Europe until the 16th century.

The first long-haired cats in this country were known as Angoras, although it cannot be positively stated that they came from Angora in Turkey. Others were supposed to have come from Persia, hence the name Persians. I presume sailors and travellers did bring them in so they might just as well have come from Persia as anywhere. Today no-one seems to know if there really were two distinct varieties, but from old descriptions there does seem to be a difference, the Angoras apparently having smaller heads, bigger ears, and longer noses. In fact, what we would refer to as 'bad or poor type', whereas the Persians had rounder heads and smaller ears. It is probable that because the early breeders preferred the look of the Persians rather than that of the Angoras, they were chosen to breed from. In my experience, although diet and living conditions help and cold weather makes the coat grow thicker, length of coat seems to be inherited, certain strains always producing kittens with very long fur.

Later, when cat-breeding became the fashion, the long-haired kittens were much admired and by choosing only the best, crossing colours, and 'making' several new varieties, the foundations were laid for the excellent Persians we have today. At the beginning of the century far more Persian cats and kittens were entered in shows than short-haired, but with growing popularity of the Siamese, the pattern changed, with more short-hairs than long-hairs. However the pattern is changing again. The Burmese are being shown in greater numbers, rivalling those of the Siamese, while the long-hairs' popularity seems to be very much on the increase, with much larger entries at the show. In fact at some shows, they number twice as many as the Siamese.

The Siamese and other foreign short-hairs are usually more prolific in size and number of litters. The average Persian litter is three to four, as opposed to the five to seven of the Siamese, although I have had six kittens in a Blue Persian litter and have heard of several with seven.

There are now 69 different varieties of pedigree cats in Britain, but these are added to from time to time as new varieties are recognized.

There are three main breeds, the British, the Foreign and the Persian or long-haired. To enable the reader to distinguish at a glance between them, briefly; The British are of sturdy build, with round heads, big eyes, thick short fur, and thick, not too long, tails. The Foreign cats have long slinky bodies, large upright ears, almond shaped eyes and long whip-like tails. The coats are short and sleek, but type and fur does vary from variety to variety. In this book we are only interested in the Persians considered by many to be the most beautiful.

Characteristics of a Persian or long-haired

The Persians are divided into a number of recognized varieties by the Governing Council of the Cat Fancy. Basically the standards of characteristics required to make a perfect specimen are the same, except in the cases of the Birman, Turkish, Balinese and Angoras, the main differences being colour, coat pattern (or lack of it), and eye colour.

A perfect Persian cat should have a round broad head with good width between the small, neat ears, a short broad nose, full round cheeks, good chin, tufted ears and big round eyes. A cobby body is required: that is, low-lying on short legs, with good bone structure. The tail should be short and very full, plume-like in appearance, not tapering to a point. The long fur thick and flowing around the head should be trained to form a frill or ruff. All varieties are supposed to conform to the standard, but some are better type than others. One hundred points are apportioned between colour, coat, body, head and eyes.

It is practically impossible to breed a perfect cat conforming in every way to the standard, but many seen at shows are wonderful animals and it is always a challenge and an aim to a breeder to try to produce a cat as near perfection as possible.

General standard of the Persians

Body: Cobby, on low thick legs.
Coat: Long, flowing and silky. Full ruff around neck.
Tail: Short and full.
Head: Round and broad, good space between ears, full cheeks. Broad muzzle, short nose with distinct stop. Bold round eyes, neat well-covered small ears.

The hundred points are apportioned between the colour, coat, body and eyes, with slight variations for each variety, e.g. for the Blue Persian head 25 points is allowed, while the Black head is allotted 20 points. The Governing Council of the Cat Fancy issue a full standard of points, covering every recognized variety.

The varieties

No.		Coat Colour	Eye Colour
1	BLACK	Lustrous raven black.	Copper or deep orange
2	WHITE	Pure white, no markings.	Deep blue
2a	WHITE	Pure white, no markings.	Orange or deep copper
2b	WHITE	Pure white, no markings.	Odd eyed
3	BLUE	Any shade of blue.	Orange or deep copper
4	RED SELF	Deep rich red.	Deep copper
5	CREAM	Pure sound cream.	Deep copper
6	SMOKE	Black shading to silver. Undercoat white.	Orange or copper
6a	BLUE SMOKE	Blue shading to silver. Undercoat white.	Orange or copper
7	SILVER TABBY	Pale silver ground. Jet black markings.	Green or hazel
8	BROWN TABBY	Rich tawny sable ground. Dense black markings.	Hazel or copper
9	RED TABBY	Deep rich red colour. Dark red markings.	Deep copper
10	CHINCHILLA	Pure white undercoat, black tickings.	Emerald or blue green
11	TORTOISESHELL	Black, red and cream well broken into patches.	Deep orange or copper
12	TORTOISESHELL AND WHITE	Black, red and cream interspersed with white.	Deep orange or copper
12a	BI-COLOUR	Any solid colour, with white.	Deep orange or copper
13	BLUE CREAM	Blue and cream softly intermingled.	Deep orange or copper
13a	ANY OTHER COLOUR (Assessment only classes)	Now any colour, any pattern.	Any colour
13b	COLOURPOINT	Seal, blue or chocolate, etc. points on cream, white or ivory respectively.	Clear bright blue
13c	BIRMAN	Seal, blue or chocolate, etc. points on slightly golden beige. 4 white paws.	Bright China blue
13d	TURKISH	Chalk white. Auburn markings.	Light amber

2

THE RECOGNIZED BREEDS

Black Persians

AN ADULT prize-winning Black Persian can be a really splendid looking animal with the long lustrous dense black coat and the large orange eyes forming a wonderful contrast. As in all long-haired varieties the body should be cobby on low legs, with powerful chest, the tail should be shortish, full and plume-like, while the broad round head should have plenty of space between the neat small ears. The large round eyes may be copper or orange while the nose should be snub and short. The long flowing coat must be of glossy jet black, pure right through to the roots. Even in the brightest of daylight a perfect black should show no brown or grey tinge and there must be no sign of bars or any other markings. This is a breed that often does not reach perfection until well after the first birthday. The kittens when born may be rusty-brown in colour but the rustiest-looking kitten in a litter may often turn out to be the best adult. It takes months for this rusty colouring and any white hairs to grow out and the coat to attain the dense blackness required in a good show specimen. Even in an adult the coat colouring varies with the seasons and for a cat to be shown it is even more important than in other long-haired varieties to choose the moment of perfection.

Blacks need careful and prolonged show preparation to enable them to look their best with gleaming jet black coats. Some breeders sprinkle the coat with a little bay rum and polish daily with a chamois leather. This will also help to remove any white or coarse hairs and give the coat a wonderful sheen. A cat that is to be shown should not be allowed to sleep in strong sunlight for long periods as the coat soon takes on a rusty hue, nor should he be allowed to roll on dusty pathways, as a Black can look dishevelled very quickly.

Black Persian kittens do not always do as well as they should at shows because of the time taken for the coat to become really black and often they are shown before they are ready. Planned breeding is essential and it may not always pay to mate black to black. If there is a loss of type when this is done, a mating with an outstanding Blue Persian may help. The best kitten of the resultant litter mated to a good Black could produce very good Blacks, and many famous black champions of the past were produced in this way. Blacks are useful as mates for the Tortoiseshell and Tortoiseshell and White females. The kittens produced from such matings could include a Black and even a Tortoiseshell. Blacks have also been used successfully in the breeding of Smokes and may also be used to endeavour to produce the really dense black markings in the Silver Tabbies, but there is the danger here that the markings may be too solid. If mated to a White, a Black may produce some good white kittens.

Over the past few years there has been renewed interest in Blacks, with some outstanding animals being exhibited. The type and eye colour is usually good, and Blacks have a number of times been Best in Show, a real achievement with so many beautiful other varieties being exhibited.

Since medieval days when the cat was hounded and persecuted, as a familiar of witches, as having close connections with the Devil and Black Magic, the Black in particular seems to have been the object of many superstitions, both for good and bad luck. The first cat I can remember having when small was a Black Persian, which slept on my bed whenever he could. I can remember being at first awed and then fascinated by the crackles and the electric sparks which came when I stroked him in the dark. I have tried this on other long-haired varieties but it seems to me the Blacks produce the most electricity. This same cat, although extremely gentle and affectionate, took on the appearance of 'the Devil's cat himself', as a neighbour said, should a dog dare to pass by, when the large orange eyes seemed to grow even bigger and every black hair stood

Opposite: Black Persians, with their contrasting orange eyes, can be splendid-looking animals, but need much attention to enable them to look their best.

on end. I have seen many dogs turn and flee rather than pass the gate and the terrifying-looking monster there.

White Persians

White Perians are now very popular, and there is a steady demand for the kittens. There are three recognized varieties, the Orange-eyed, the Blue-eyed, and the Odd-eyed, with one eye blue and the other orange. The Orange-eyed and the Blue-eyed, the latter being the original colour, appeared in the same class at the cat shows, with the Odd-eyed not being shown. As the Orange-eyed can be bred successfully from Black, Cream or a Blue mated to a White, the type of this variety was infinitely better than that of the Blue-eyed, and they invariably won, and eventually both eye-colours were recognized. More recently the Odd-eyed were also recognized, given a class of their own, and now have championship status.

Apart for the eye colouring, the standard required is as for the other Persians, a cobby body with long flowing silky coat of purest white with no black hairs, shadings or signs of markings. There must be no yellow staining. The small ears on the round broad head should be well tufted, the nose short and broad, the chin strong, the cheeks well developed. Unfortunately, until recently the Blue-eyed failed somewhat in type, this being difficult to improve without losing the eye colour, the nose being a little too long and the ears too tall, the body inclined to be long and rangy, but as more breeders have become interested in the White Persians more thought has been given to pedigree and breeding. The results are gratifying, the type being vastly improved and the body more cobby. The Orange-eyed variety should have eyes of deep orange or copper, large and round, while the eyes of the Blue should be really deep blue, not at all wishy-washy. The Odd-eyed should have one deep blue eye and one deep orange.

There is an element of deafness which affects some white cats, more especially those with blue eyes, although all with eyes of that colour are not necessarily deaf. The Orange-eyed Whites are rarely deaf, and the Odd-eyed are occasionally deaf on the blue eyed side and not on the orange. Even if they are deaf, they appear very sensitive to their surroundings and react to vibrations. They are invariably highly intelligent and the deafness is not the terrible handicap it might be expected to be. I would not recommend having a deaf cat living in a busy road with much traffic, but for pets who seldom go out or live in the country, there will be plenty of enjoyment in life. The deafness appears to be inherited to a certain extent and if thought is given when mating, only using cats with good hearing, it may be possible in time to eradicate the risk.

The Odd-eyed variety is most useful in a breeding programme, as it may be used to produce all three White varieties. The kittens when born present rather a fragile appearance particularly the blue-eyed variety, as the coat is so short, they look almost pinkish, but often the kitten with the most naked look develops the best coat when maturity is reached. There should be no black hairs but

Orange-eyed White Persians, like all the whites, are intelligent and sensitive and given to keeping themselves spotlessly clean.

often a few appear, particularly on the head, and strangely enough if blue-eyed, the kittens so marked may not suffer from deafness. It is difficult to assess the eye colour of the kittens as all are born with blue eyes, but if the blue is pale as a kitten, there will never be the deep sapphire colouring required. If orange-eyed, the colour will start to change when about five or six weeks and will gradually change from blue to grey and then to deep orange. The Odd-eyed will be easier to assess.

Many people are hesitant about taking on a white cat, especially long-haired, feeling that they will have to spend much time grooming and keeping them clean, but this is not usually found necessary. My experience is that whites manage to keep themselves spotless. Of course they need as much grooming as do the other long-haired cats, grease marks and stains showing up and any yellow staining on the tail being particularly noticeable. Their coats can be kept clean by daily powdering with good talcum powder and plenty of brushing. One or two breeders advocate bathing but great care must be taken over this as some cats catch cold easily. Warm water with a baby or poodle shampoo may be used to make a good lather and no soap must be left in the coat at all as it will have a dull appearance. Several rinsings are required, the last one having, perhaps, just a touch of blue in it. No water must be allowed to get into the ears or eyes and the fur must be dried thoroughly, the cat being kept in the warm and away from draughts until the coat is absolutely dry and fluffy again. If the tail alone has yellow or dirty stains on it, it may not be necessary to bath the whole cat. By sitting the animal on the draining board, and I have done this with my stud, the tail may be immersed gently in a jug of soapy lather, thoroughly rinsed and dried. Males in particular seem to suffer with stained and even scurfy tails. If a cat is to be bathed ready for a show, I think it is better to do this a few days before-hand rather than the day prior to the show as it gives the coat a chance to get back some of the natural oil, and powdering, brushing and combing carefully and thoroughly the day before can produce a really wonderful pure sparkling white full coat. As the cat is white, do make sure that all the powder has been removed from the coat before judging as although it may not be seen, if clouds of powder arise when handled, the judge may disqualify. Never powder in the actual show hall as this, too, may cause disqualification.

Blue Persians

I have been breeding Blue Persians for thirty years and have been asked several times if I do find it monotonous always having the same coloured litters time after time. Before I started really serious breeding I had a number of varieties of long hairs, including Black, Brown Tabby, Silver Tabbies and others, Although all these have really delightful kittens, I never found the demand for them in those days that there were for the Blue Persians and any one coming to buy a kitten always chose a Blue if there was one available. So I gradually cut down the number of my cats from twenty of various varieties to six of the best Blues I could afford. I have found that a small number of cats having their freedom breed better and are definitely more prolific than a large number kept in a cattery. Blue Persians respond as much as or even more so than other cats to individual care and attention, each liking to feel that he or she is the pet of the house. I am fortunate in living in a fairly secluded position with no neighbours and the cats can climb, play and run about as they wish, frequently popping in to have a word with me to make sure I am still here.

There is certainly nothing monotonous in having only Blue Persian kittens. To me, from the time of birth every kitten is an individual. One will spit and swear at me when only an hour or two old if I dare to touch him; another will purr with pleasure as she pads away at her mother's side; yet another, when only two days old, will really fight the others to get to his chosen spot. I find it possible to tell each one apart from birth. There is always some variation even at that age, in the shape of the head, the set of the ears, the length of the tail, and the depth of the tabby markings. No, that isn't a mistake. They really do have shadow tabby markings. These fade with the growth of the coat and often the most marked becomes the palest in the litter. The average number in a litter appears to be about four, each kitten developing an entirely different character although having identical attention and upbringing. One will be really naughty, jumping on the others, eating from his sister's dish, biting his mother's tail, while another will hang back with an 'I'm shy' expression, will arch his back and swear at strangers, while yet another brother is weaving in and out of the visitors' legs, purring with pleasure. There is certainly plenty of variety and fun in each litter.

In the 1880's the Blue Persians were shown under the 'Any Other Variety' classification, and indeed many appeared to have markings and white patchings. By the 1890's the Blues had their own classes and were fast becoming the most popular breed. The colourings seemed to have been good with such apt description as a coat the colour of 'wet blue slate' or 'the blue of smoke', but the old photographs show cats with long straight noses and large upright ears. The eyes were sometimes green and even now some of the cats shown occasionally have a green rim to their copper eyes, which is a bad fault.

Thinking about the first Blues, I realize how much foresight and care has been used over the years until now a good Blue champion is one of the best examples of how a Persian should look, conforming closely to the set standard. This is for a cobby body on low legs, with broad round head, small well-set, well-tufted ears, a short broad nose and full round cheeks. Any shade from dark to pale blue is permissible but fashions change and the paler kittens seem to fetch a better price. Whatever the colour blue, it must be sound right down to the roots without shadiness and with no white hairs, which frequently do appear.

Blue Persians from Britain have a world-wide reputation and have been exported to most parts of the world, including Persia (now Iran,) where there were said to have been long-haired blue cats many centuries ago, but I cannot imagine the type and coat quality was anything like ours, which are purely the result of selective breeding. In the past, by using a Blue male, the poor type has been much improved in other varieties, which often failed in this.

Grooming plays an important part in the preparation of a Blue for a show (see the chapter on grooming). The blue fur reacts strongly to sunlight, any old hairs in the coat particularly going quite brown. I didn't realize how much so until the one year we did have a good summer, I was asked where I had got my Brown Persian from. I realized that my very pale Blue male had been out in the sun so much that his coat was completely sunburnt. Often the old hairs along the spine and down the tail go almost black and quite hard brushing and combing is necessary to get them to fall out. I find that the kittens with the very pale coats turn brownish with the constant licking of the mother. Mine especially, as the other cats look after one another's litters as well as their own, and it is a wonder sometimes that the poor babies don't get washed away.

Red Self Persians

This is a most difficult variety to breed. The type may be very good, the body being cobby and the head round with small ears, but often stripes, bars and markings appear particlarly on the head. The coat should be deep rich red and the eyes of deep copper.

It is worthwhile mating a promising Red Self female to one of the self-coloured varieties to get away from the stripes, as though it may help the colour to use a Red Tabby, there is the danger of introducing stripes again which would prove most difficult to breed out. I have had a Red Self here for stud. Mated to my Blue Persian she produced two very nice Tortoiseshells, a Blue and one Red Self.

Cream Persians

To breed a cat with perfect type, cobby, full tail, low thick legs and a broad round head with neat ears, the colour of Devonshire cream, with large deep copper-colour eyes is the aim of every Cream breeder. It is very difficult to breed such an animal, but as the result of selective breeding many good examples with outstanding type may be seen at the shows, running the popular Blue Persian very close.

At the beginning of the century there was a recognized standard for Fawn or Cream Persians but there seems to have been far more Fawn-coated cats with almond shaped eyes than the pale Cream with big orange eyes, and it is the early members of the Cat Fancy we should thank today, who by careful thought and choosing only the cats with the creamiest coats and the roundest eyes to breed from, are really responsible for the popularity this breed has today.

A Cream should have a pale to medium cream coloured coat with no tint or shadings, or white undercoat, the colour being even right through to the roots. There must be no signs of darker bars or tabby markings anywhere, nor must the tummy be of a paler shade than the back. It is not easy to breed the exact colour required, too pale is as bad as too dark. Very often there tends to be a reddish tinge referred to as 'hot' along the spine, with the hair there being a little coarser than the rest of the the coat. A white tip to the tail is also a bad fault. Cream may be mated to a Cream but to do so indefinitely may produce kittens of too hot a shade or deterioration in type. To use a Blue stud may help to keep the type but not necessarily the colour of the first generation. However, such a mating will produce Cream males and Blue-Cream females, and if these Blue-Creams are mated back to a Cream male, very good Cream kittens may result. In the pages on Blue-Creams may be found fuller details of possible Cream matings and the kittens produced.

Brown Tabbies

One of my first pedigree kittens many years ago was a Brown Tabby Persian from a well-known breeder and since then I have always had a fondness for this variety. I knew very little about pedigree cats or indeed any cats, but looking back I think the brown was a real rich sable, better than many of this variety exhibited today. When one speaks of a tabby, many are surprised to learn that there are pedigree tabbies, thinking of the thousands of mongrel cats seen around with striped patterns of some sort or another, the word 'tabby' having been used for centuries for any cat with any form of stripes or blotches, from the pattern on silken material which originally came from the Attabiya district of Baghdad. Although many cats have markings and stripes, to breed a pedigree Brown Tabby with the pattern conforming to the standard required, particularly with the long hair, is quite difficult, even just to get the required brown—a rich tawny sable. The markings should be black, delicately pencilled on the face and dense along the back, down the sides, under the stomach, the tail ringed and the legs striped. The markings on the shoulders should form a butterfly with rings on the chest and a Lord Mayor's chain or necklace around the neck. A bad fault is white hairs. Often the chin is white and the tip of the tail, there are white hairs in the coat or the coat is brindled with dark hairs appearing in the brown.

Studying old show reports and photographs seems to show that the old Brown Tabbies were better than many of those bred in recent years. There are some good ones, but I notice that the numbers do not increase. Ironically, perhaps, it is because the kittens are so sweet and attractive in appearance, they sell well and become neutered pets, which does not help to increase the breeding numbers. A Tabby queen I had when mated to my Blue stud always produced a very nice Brown Tabby kitten in the litter, and without fail this was invariably the first to be sold. They are very intelligent, most affectionate and fascinating. Mating Brown Tabby to Brown Tabby, if both are of good type and with good markings, should produce nice kittens but in order to improve the type and possibly the denseness of the markings, an outstanding Black would make a good mate. The markings must be distinct and dense black standing out from the brown background.

Silver Tabbies

A good Silver Tabby has a ground coat of shining silver with the black markings forming a wonderful contrast. Because of the long coat, unless the markings are really dense they do not show up as well as in the short-haired variety. The markings should conform to a definite pattern, with butterfly markings on the shoulders, with deep bands on the saddle and the sides, with two necklaces or 'Lord Mayor's' chains around the neck, swirls on the cheeks, bracelets around the legs, spectacles around the eyes, 'M' mark on the forehead, and a ringed tail. Unfortunately, brindling often occurs, with silver appearing in the black markings, spoiling the appearance.

I have had both long- and short-haired and it really is difficult to breed a long-haired Silver Tabby with absolutely correct markings. I find that in the long-haired the markings often have a smudged appearance. Silver Tabby may be mated to Silver Tabby but in time the type and markings deteriorate. Mating to a black Persian may help to darken the stripes but there is always the danger that the markings will become too solid.

Old books mention that the Silver Tabby was used to produce the fairy-like Chinchillas. I have found the Silvers very intelligent, fond of their home and owner, loving their kittens intensely, and always looking most ornamental.

Red Tabby Persians

There is a common fallacy that all Red Tabbies are male. This is untrue. A Red Tabby is often sired by a male Red and a female Tortoiseshell, in which case any Red kittens born will probably be male, but if breeding is pure Red on both sides, a Red Tabby male and female can be mated together to produce both Red Tabby males and females but there may be more males. Mating Red to Red indefinitely is not a good plan. So often the colour seems to fade, the markings become indistinct and the type is not always good. A useful outcross is a Black of outstanding type. The colour

The Silver Tabby, with its coat of shining silver and contrasting black markings, always looks most ornamental—as this kitten kindly demonstrates.

should be a deep rich copper red with darker red markings standing out distinctly, forming a butterfly on the shoulder, with clear markings on the face, two rings across the chest, and bands on the saddle and sides. The large eyes should be of deep copper. There must be no white anywhere. So often white appears on the chin and on the tip of the tail. The tummy must not be paler than the rest of the coat. A good Red Tabby with the deep rich colouring always attracts a great deal of attention and seems to be favoured particularly by men. There can be no comparison with the sandy and ginger pet cats usually known as 'marmalade' cats.

Smokes
This is one of the most striking and distinctive of the long-haired

The Black Smoke, although one of the most striking and distinctive of varieties, often does not reveal its true characteristics until the adult stage is reached, when the white undercoat shows like silver through the dense black top coat.

varieties, but the newly-born kittens give little indication of the beauty that may be theirs when older. They are usually black with no signs of the contrasting silver required, for not until the adult stage is reached does a Smoke have the required white undercoat, showing like silver through the dense black silky top coat.

Breeders hesitate to register the kittens at too early an age as often the blackest kitten turns out to be the best cat and it may be nearly a year old before the real Smoke may be truly appreciated. The standard requires the body colour to be black with silver on the sides and flanks. The mask, or the face colouring, should be black with the frill and ear tufts of silver. The type required is as in all the long-hairs and is frequently very good, particularly when a good Black Persian has been used as a stud. Smoke may be bred to Smoke but eventually this may be detrimental to type and possibly may also mean loss of the deep orange or copper eye colouring, so it is good to use a Black occasionally. A Blue Persian may also be used as a stud but although the resultant Blue Smoke is attractive, the colouring to me is not nearly so striking as in the Black Smoke, although both types are recognized. It is not a good thing to use a Silver Tabby as a stud, as invariably stripes will appear in the progeny.

Although it was one of the earliest recognized varieties, appearing at shows as early as the end of the last century, the numbers have not increased to a very great extent, due possibly, I think, to the nondescript appearance sometimes of the young kittens. A Smoke at a cat show attracts a great deal of attention and I am glad to say that there are now several breeders trying to increase the numbers. Smokes are usually very affectionate, much attached to their owners and very intelligent.

Chinchillas

This is truly a case of the ugly duckling turning into a beautiful swan, if I may use this metaphor in connection with cats, as the Chinchilla kittens are so dark when born, often with Tabby markings, that sometimes it is difficult to see any indication of the truly enchanting appearance of the adult Chinchilla cat. With a pure white undercoat, delicately tipped with black on the back, sides, head, ears and tail, a neat little brick-red nose, and the wonderful emerald or blue-green black-rimmed eyes, the Chinchilla is one of the loveliest of the long-haired breeds, often being chosen as the Best Exhibit in Show. The ticking must be even with any completely black hairs or black patches being a bad fault. Yellowish stains may appear particularly on the tail and careful grooming is essential to keep a perfectly immaculate appearance. Some breeders bath as for the White, afterwards making sure that the undercoat is groomed upwards so as to make the black ticking stand well from the body, giving the cat a sparkling appearance.

I am sometimes asked why 'Chinchilla'? Frankly I dont know. It was the name given by the early breeders, who produced the breed, known in the early days as Silver Persians, by careful selection. There is certainly no similarity between these fairy-like cats and the popular little rodent Chinchillas now being produced for their fur, or the rabbits with similar names.

Chinchilla kittens are so dark when born that they do not seem to herald the enchanting appearance of the adult cat which is often chosen as the Best Exhibit in Show.

The Tortoiseshell and White

To my mind this is one of the most striking of the long-haired breeds, the bright patches of red, cream and black, with white on the face, the chest and stomach, the legs and the paws making a very attractive cat. In America it is known as the calico cat because of the bright colours. Although it is possible to breed cats of good type with the colours required, it is far from easy to breed one with the true coat pattern. The colours should be evenly distributed all over the body with white in the correct places only and not too much of it. The black, red and cream patches must be distinct and in no way intermingled or blurred, and there must be no brindling (that is, hairs of a different colouring in the patches). Too often a bad fault is the appearance of tabby markings spoiling the whole appearance of the cat. This may be due to perhaps using a Red Tabby in an endeavour to improve the red patches, but introduc-

The Tortoiseshell and White, or calico cat, is almost always a female whose affectionate and highly intelligent kittens make very attractive pets.

ing tabby markings is a bad thing as they are extremely difficult to breed out and may even appear generations after. The Tortie and White is nearly always a female. Like the Tortoiseshell, a so-called male is always cropping up but invariably proves to be a difficult-to-sex female, and the one or two males that are born, being sterile.

In the past the breeding of this variety was unpredictable, with various matings being tried to produce them. Comparatively recently, however, by using Red and White or Black and White bi-colour males of good type, and having Tortie and White breeding, it has been found possible to produce litters with some Tortie and White kittens. Outstanding Tortie and White kittens fetch good prices and usually sell readily. Even if the markings are not quite correct, these affectionate and highly intelligent kittens make very attractive pets.

The standard required is the same as for the other Persians, that is a massive cobby body on low legs, with round broad head, tiny well-placed ears, good broad nose and full cheeks. The big eyes may be deep orange or copper. Grooming is also important, especially if the cat is to be shown. Daily brushing and combing is necessary, the undercoat being made to stand well away instead of clinging to the body, as this will show the brilliant colouring to the best advantage. Particular attention should be given to the tail which must be brushed out to its full width.

The Tortoiseshells

The name 'Tortoiseshell' is applied rather indiscriminantly to any cat having black, cream and red in its coat, but a really good Tortoiseshell bred to the required Persian standard has to have the three colours in clear separate patches without white hairs or smudging of the colours. This is difficult to achieve in the long flowing coat. The Tortie is full of personality, invariably female. Although there are many tales of valuable males worth a small fortune, I am afraid I must disillusion readers. Males have appeared occasionally but are usually incapable of siring. Others thought to be males when born turn out to be females and produce kittens of their own. The female must be mated to a self-coloured variety. It is difficult to predict the resultant litter. Certainly the kittens will be most interesting, probably of varied colours, and

given great luck there may be a tortoiseshell among them. The kittens when born are usually almost black with only slight suggestions of the black, cream and red patches to come. Often the darkest kitten will become the best marked adult. The patches must be bright and clear, well broken, clearly defined and entirely separate, and evenly distributed. The head colouring is important. A red or cream blaze, or splash, that is the mark down the centre of the head, running from the nose, is liked and gives a distinctive look to the face. The type is usually good. The patches must not be too big, and be clear with no white hairs or brindling. The coat must be long and flowing, and it is very important that in the long hair the patches show up distinctively. It is easier to see the correct patching in the short-haired variety, and it is a real achievement to breed a good long-haired Tortie with the three colours in more or less equal proportions as black tends to dominate. Correct grooming is essential to make the undercoat stand up and thus make the pattern flow. One can never state with certainty that one is going to be a breeder of Tortoiseshells as it may be many litters before one appears, if at all. It is not always necessary to use a Tortie to produce one, as a Red Self mated to my Blue stud produced a Blue, a Red, and two beautiful little Tortoiseshell kittens. These two looked really black when born, only having one or two small colour patches on the head and body, and it was many weeks before the owner realized that she had two Tortie kittens. A self-coloured Persian is the best stud as to use any tabby may introduce stripes.

The Tortoiseshell is one of the oldest breeds known. They have a good reputation as mousers and ratters and even today both the long- and short-haired varieties may be found on many farms. They are good mothers, fond of their kittens, but not over-indulgent, and teach them independence at an early age.

Bicolours

Cats with two-coloured coats, *viz* a solid colour with white, were often seen at the very early cat shows, but were usually short-

Opposite: The Tortoiseshell Persian, with the colours black, cream and red in its coat in clear separate patches, is also almost always female.

White and Red and White and Black Bicolour Persians.

coated. Of more recent years, long-hairs with coats of two colours were frequently produced from varying matings; were registered as Any Other Colour, and were shown in that class.

Eventually it was realized that Bicolours were useful in the breeding of Tortie and Whites, and recognition was given. However, the standard required, being similar to that of the Dutch rabbit was so specific, requiring such definite colour divisions, that it proved impossible to reproduce in cats. In 1971, this was modified, and it was agreed that the coats could be of any solid colours with white, with not more than two-thirds of the coat to be coloured, and not more than half to be white. The patches of colour to be clear and well distributed, with the face also to be patched with the colour and white. The type is as for most other long-hairs; the heads being broad and round, with short noses, small ears, and big orange or copper eyes.

Opposite: Red and White Bicolour Persian kitten, looking pensive.

Bicolours may be mated to bicolours, but to keep the type it may be necessary to use a self-coloured stud occasionally. Cross-breeding may also result in kittens with tri-coloured coats, which are recognized, and are exhibited in the Tortie and White classes.

Blue Cream Persians

I consider this one of the most difficult varieties to breed to conform to the required standard which calls for a cat with a 'softly intermingled' coat of pastel blue and cream. A Blue Cream may have exceptionally good type but so often the coat has a patched effect. This is permitted in North America but would go against a cat in this country.

Blue Creams may be produced by a Tortoiseshell mating with a Blue or even a Black, but more usually by the mating of a Blue and a Cream. Such matings may produce cats of exceptional type and a good eye colour and sometimes, but not always, the desired misty look. Often too reddish a tinge may appear on the coat and there may be small cream patches on the paws and head. A blaze or strip of colour in the centre of the head is liked by some breeders although not in the standard.

The Blue Cream is nearly always a female, the very rare male being sterile, but by using a Blue or a Cream stud it is possible to get delightful variation in the litters, as follows:

Cream female mated to Blue male	Cream male kittens
	Blue Cream females
Cream male mated to a Blue female	Blue males
	Blue Cream females
Blue Cream female mated to a Cream male	Blue Cream females
	Cream males
	Cream females
	Blue males
Blue Cream female mated to a Blue male	Cream males
	Blue males
	Blue females
	Blue Cream females

Opposite: Colourpoint Blue, a Persian with the colour pattern of the recognised Siamese.

The Colourpoint Long-Hair

The Colourpoint is a made breed, and is the result of years of selective breeding, patience and a great deal of money being spent. Many people in several countries, including Sweden, America and Britain tried by experimental breeding, crossing and discarding to produce such an animal and Mr. Stirling Webb in this country was most successful in producing this wonderful variety with Siamese colourings and the Persian coat.

The Colourpoint has the coat pattern of the Siamese, that is, in the case of the Seal Point, a Cream coat with wonderfully-contrasting points of a dark seal brown. The eyes too are the blue of the Siamese, but there any resemblance to this breed ceases, as the type is definitely long-haired. The head should be broad and round with small neat ears, the body cobby and the tail short and full. It is possible to reproduce the colour pattern of any of the recognized Siamese, that is cream, with cream body colour; blue, with glacial-white body colour; chocolate with ivory body colour; lilac, with magnolia; red with off-white; Tortie with cream body; and also cream, blue-cream, chocolate cream and lilac-cream points. A blaze is liked in the Tortic-points, which is invariably a female-only variety.

This variety has proved very popular, so much so, that there is now a show for Colourpoints alone.

Birmans

This is a variety that differs from most other long-hairs in that in addition to having the coat pattern of the Siamese, a light body colouring with contrasting points, it has the very distinctive feature of four white-gloved paws. It is said to have originated in Burma centuries ago, but more recently has been known in France. Another theory is that it was produced by cross-breeding between Siamese and long-hairs.

The type differs too. The heads are not so broad as other long-hairs; the bodies are long and low; the tails are not so short, and the fur not so luxurious. The white back gauntlets should finish in a

Opposite: Colourpoint Seal, with its wonderfully-contrasting points of dark seal brown.

point up the back of the legs, while the front gloves should just cover the paws. The eyes should be bright blue.

They are being bred with seal, blue, chocolate and lilac points, with appropriate body colouring, but it is possible to produce them with other point colourings, as given for the Siamese and Colourpoints.

They are cats with charming personalities, and proving very popular. First introduced into Britain from France, they are being bred by a number of fanciers, and have been exported to all parts of the world.

Turkish
Known in Turkey for centuries, the Turkish cats were introduced into Britain from the Van area in the 1950's. Their build is similar to the first Angoras ever seen in Europe, that is the heads are short wedges, with large ears and long noses, the sturdy bodies long, and full, medium-length tails. The fur is chalk-white, with attractive auburn markings on the face, and the tails being ringed with the same colour. The eyes should be light amber in colour.

When first introduced into Britain, they gained fame through being referred to as the swimming cats, as it was known that in Turkey they would swim of their own accord in warm shallow pools and streams. All cats can swim when necessary, but few choose to swim unless they have to.

The original pair proved to breed true, and several more were imported, but the numbers have not increased to any great extent. They have been exported to other parts of the world, where they attract much attention at the shows.

Any Other Colour (Assessment)
Until recently there was in Britain a classification Any Other Colour. This was for cats with colours, markings or coat pattern not conforming to the one of the recognized varieties. Cats and kittens were registered as such, and were entered in these classes at the shows. The classes were useful for entering cats resulting from experimental breeding or mis-mating, but it was not satisfactory to the serious breeders, in that no championships could be given, and the winners were purely judge's choice.

A number of new varieties are in the process of being produced, many the result of years of carefully planned breeding, and it was realized by the Governing Council of the Cat Fancy that some new way of judging them was desirable. It was decided that a more fair way of judging these cats would be by a provisional standard put forward by the particular clubs interested in the varieties; that the cats would not compete against one another, but each exhibit would be assessed individually by three separate judges at a show. Special Assessment forms are now provided, with headings such as head, body shape, coat, etc. with the judge writing in her opinion on such characteristics, going by the provisional standard displayed on the pen. If considered worthy, each judge could award a merit certificate, or if not up to standard, could withhold this.

In due course application may be made for a recognized standard and championship status, when pure breeding, the number of merits awarded, the numbers of variety bred, and the number of fanciers producing them would all be taken into consideration. Should recognition be given, the cats may be re-registered as such and would then have an Open Class at the show, with eventually championships being granted.

There are a number of long-hairs now appearing in the Assessment classes, the majority of which will undoubtedly be given breed numbers in due course.

I received a telephone call some time ago from an excited owner saying that, in a mixed litter, her cat had produced a beautifully marked long-haired kitten different from anything she had ever seen. It was red with white markings and she knew that many would like to buy one like it and she would like to 'make' such a breed. I am afraid one cannot start a new breed just like that. As the cat in question had got out and the father was unknown, the chance of her ever having another kitten with the same colouring and identical markings is very remote.

To produce a new or 'made' breed, particularly in the long-hairs, means long term planning, sometimes involving the use of short-haired cats if a certain colour is required, the discarding and selling as pets the kittens with too short a coat and the wrong colour, and using only those with the best type. The eye colouring is very important and may take time to breed true. Incorrect markings may keep popping up and that is the reason why the Governing Council of the Cat Fancy insist on receiving details of three generations of breeding true before they will consider the recognition of a new variety and many merit awards.

The much admired Colourpoint Long-Hair was the result of such planning by Mr. Stirling Webb, the well-known breeder. His was the particularly hard task to set the Siamese colourings in a long coat and to get the vivid blue of the Siamese eye into the round eye of the Persian.

A short description of those with provisional standards now appearing in the assessment classes follows:

Angoras.   The original long-hairs seen in Euope were said to be the Angoras, which came from Angora, now Ankara in Turkey. These cats had long, tapering wedge-shaped heads, long noses, large ears and almond-shaped eyes; the bodies were of medium size, but long and dainty; the legs were long, and the tails long and tapering. The cats from Persia had different type, the heads were broader and the eyes bigger, and these were preferred. The Angoras gradually died out, but a few years ago the United States imported cats from Turkey with the original Angora type. They are recognized there, and are being bred in a number of colours and coat patterns. They are now appearing in Britain, with identical type, and may be seen in the assessment classes. The fur is silky and long, but not so flowing as in most other long-hairs.

Balinese.   This variety has been recognized in the United States for a few years, and has now made its appearance in Britain. They have the coat pattern and colourings of the Siamese, and longish fine silky fur. Unlike the Colourpoints, these cats have typical Siamese type, with wedge-shaped heads, large pointed ears, oriental-shaped blue eyes, long bodies and long thin tails.

They are being bred with seal, chocolate, blue and lilac points, but may also be produced in other point colourings recognized in the Siamese.

Chocolate and Lilac Long-hairs.   It was the Colourpoint selective breeding that produced the Chocolate and the Lilacs as long ago as the early 1960's, but at the time few were interested in breeding them. It has proved very difficult to improve the type and eye colouring, which should be deep orange or copper. Lilac is a dilute form of Brown, and will never be confused with the Blue, being an entirely different hue. The cats being shown in the Assessment classes have now much better type and colouring.

From the cross-breeding required to improve the varieties, cats with Chocolate Tortoiseshell and Lilac Cream colouring have also been produced. These are female-only varieties.

Cameos. As far as is known the first Cameos were developed in the 1950's by crossing Smokes and Tortoiseshellls. Over the years a number of different matings were tried, including Reds, Silvers and Chinchillas.

The type required is as for most other long-hairs, with broad heads, tiny ears, and copper round eyes. The variations are as follows:

Shell Cameo or Red Chinchilla
Shaded Cameo or Red Shaded
Smoke cameo or Red Smoke
Cameo Tabby
Shell and Shaded Tortoiseshell Cameos, female-only varieties.

The Shell should have red tippings, with white undercoat, while the Shaded has more heavy tippings, and the Smoke should appear as a red, until on movement the white undercoat shows through. The Cameo Tabby should have red markings on the white undercoat, while the Shell and Shaded Tortie should have well-defined patches of red cream and black tipping, with white undercoat

The Cameos are appearing in the Assessment classes, and will doubtless be recognized in the near future.

Shaded Silver. Although this is a very old variety, it has not been recognized in Britain for many years, as at the beginning of the century the Chinchillas were far from being the delicately tipped dainty cats we know today, some being much heavily tipped than others. Some were known as Chinchillas and some as Shaded Silvers, and it proved difficult to know which was which, so the Shaded variety was dropped. In America and other parts of the world, however, they are still recognized, and they are now appearing in the assessment classes in Britain.

They appear in the same litter as the Chinchillas, and as the kittens all have tabby markings when tiny, it may be difficult to decide which is which at first. In the Shaded the tippings should take the form of a mantle gradually shading down the sides; the undercoat should be white. The eyes should be sea-green, and the type as for the Chinchillas; the fur long and flowing.

Pewters.   Another new variety seen in the Assessment classes are the Pewters, once referred to as Blue Chinchillas, with the coats being a silver-white, evenly shaded with black, giving the effect of a mantle as in the Shaded Silvers. The great difference is in the eye colouring which should be orange or copper. The type is as for the Chinchillas, and the fine silk fur long and flowing.

3

CHOOSING A KITTEN

ONCE YOU have decided that you want a Persian kitten, your first inclination will probably be to buy the first kitten you hear about regardless of colour, condition or where it comes from. Please exercise patience and take time and thought over your choice. Think well over the particular variety you favour the most, and then having made up your mind I recommend visiting Cat shows, not to buy one straight from the show, but to meet the breeders of the variety you are looking for and also to see the kittens in the flesh. You may be able to book one for a later date, but if you see one you like at the show, and it does not live too far away, arrange to collect it in about three weeks' time as it will then be known to be free of any possible infections. If you do buy direct from a show, make sure that the kitten has been inoculated against Infectious Feline Enteritis and ask the breeder what you should do when returning home to make sure that the small creature does not contract a chill. *Fur and Feather*, a weekly paper, carries advertisements for both cat shows and kittens. Kittens may be ordered and sent by train, but do remember to enquire the age before you confirm the deal. A kitten is regarded as such to the age of nine months, and as most people think of kittens as tiny things, several people I have known have received a shock to receive what appeared to them to be a full-grown cat. Ten to twelve weeks old is a suitable age to have your new kitten. By then he should be completely weaned, house-trained and self-reliant.

If not required for breeding, the pedigree is not all that important, and what you need is a healthy, sturdy kitten, full of life with bright wide-open, and not running eyes, clean ears, and an alert look. The fluffy coat should stand well away from the body, without clinging, and when blown gently aside there should be no signs of flea dirts or fleas. The tummy should be soft, not hard, and there should be no pot-belliedness, as this can be a sign of worms. The little tail should be held proudly upright and there should be no signs of messiness underneath it.

When the kitten arrives at his new home, he may be nervous and apprehensive, missing his mother, the other kittens, and all the familiar smells and sounds. Everything will be strange to him, even you. Talk to him quietly. Allow him to walk around the room and explore, first making sure that all the windows are closed and he cannot get up the chimney. Someone I know took his new kitten to his ground floor London home and left it in the room alone. Alas it was never seen again. The window had been left open about 4in. at the bottom and it must have climbed out. Despite all enquiries and advertisements it was never discovered what had happened.

Please do not keep picking the kitten up and nursing him. If you have children explain to them that he wants to get to know his new home, and when he has thoroughly explored the place, he will be very tired and will then be quite happy to go to sleep on someone's lap. He must be allowed to choose whose. Tell the children they must never fight over the kitten, squeeze or hold him too tightly as he is only a baby and can easily be hurt. Don't keep offering him little drops of milk or pieces of meat. A kitten can be overfed very quickly and can suffer from digestive troubles. The breeder will probably have given you a diet sheet, and for the first week or two at least try to keep to it. He may not eat much the first day because of the newness of everything.

When the kitten has explored all around, show him the sanitary tin, and also his bowl of clean drinking water. Keep the tin in the same place and he will always go to that spot, and there should not be any accidents.

If you have other cats or a dog, introduce carefully and do not make too much fuss of the newcomer as cats can be very jealous. After a few days, I usually find that older cats, especially neuters, accept kittens with very little trouble and become very attached to them.

4

GENERAL CARE, FEEDING AND MANAGEMENT

THERE IS an erroneous idea that Persian cats are delicate and therefore need cosseting and looking after more than most cats. This is quite wrong. Commonsense is essential, no over-fussing, a good mixed diet, exercise in the house if no garden is available, and love and care of your kitten should give you a happy healthy cat who will be your faithful companion for many years. Although in this book I give details for the welfare and well-being of cats, the more I have to do with them and the longer I know them, I realise that each cat is an individual and it is impossible to make or to give hard and fast rules as to what one should do or not do for a cat, as they vary so much in their likes and dislikes, their habits and characters, the food and the amount of it they will eat, their general behaviour and degree of intelligence.

Once your kitten has arrived and settled down in his new home, it will be time to start his training. I do not mean only house—but general training as well. Most kittens are very clean and arrive already used to using a sanitary tray. If you have a garden and want your kitten to give up using a tray in time, start by moving the tray slightly each day until, weather providing, it is near the door. Take him out around the garden with you, encouraging him to use the earth. Put him out several times during the day and in time he will go on his own. It may be necessary to provide a tray at night.

The breeder should have given you a diet sheet. This should be strictly adhered to for the first week or two, increasing slightly as the kitten grows. Introduce any new item in small quantities and watch for ill-effects.

Provide a basket or cardboard box with a warm blanket as sleeping quarters. My cats always prefer cardboard boxes to baskets although naturally they are not very ornamental around the house. At first the kitten will need plenty of sleep as he will be growing fast, but he will also want regular exercise, not, like a dog, being taken for walks, but he will appreciate your playing with him. Throwing a small table tennis ball, trailing string with a feather on the end, jumping on a stuffed mouse thrown around, or even catching a crumpled up paper ball will give him his necessary exercise. Most of my cats are great retrievers and will bring back time and time again any paper balls. Let him play in the garden in the sunshine.

Please if you are away from home all day do not buy a small kitten and leave it on its own all day. It is unfair as he will be miserable, lonely, and may pine. Wait until you can be home with him or try to get two older ones. They won't like it but will be more philosophical about it, and will have one another for company.

As the kitten grows older he will know instinctively the time for his meals and come and worry you if you are late. Try and keep to the same routine, feeding, grooming, and playing with him at about the same time each day.

Train him carefully. Remember: any amusing little tricks he may have as a kitten, such as crawling up a trouser leg, will not be so funny when he is much bigger. Do not let him sharpen his claws on the furniture. Provide a scratching post or log, or tree in the garden and teach him to use it. Remember grass is important to his well-being as a preventative for 'furball'. If you have none in the garden, grow some in a pot.

I give details for feeding a very young kitten in the section on litters, but the following diet may be of some help for the older kitten and fully-grown cat:

10–12 weeks. Four small meals a day.
Breakfast. A milky feed, e.g. Lactol with Scotts Baby Food or Farex/Little bread and milk/Porridge.
Mid-morning. Scraped beef, cooked rabbit, chicken or fish, mixed with a few cornflakes.
Mid-afternoon. Another milky feed.
Evening. Fish if meat in the morning or the other way round.

This may be reversed, starting with the fuller meal and finishing with milk in the evening. The meals may be cut down to three with increased quantities until by the age of six months the cat is having three meals a day, a full breakfast, a mid-day milky feed, and an evening full meal. By nine months the meals may be two a day, morning and evening, although my cats have goat's milk mid-day as well.

I give below some of the items which will provide a good varied diet. Never stick to one item. Provide as much variation as possible, e.g. too much fish can be the cause of eczema, particularly in the long-haired cats. I always mix any food with a few corn flakes or a little brown bread.

Raw beef
Cooked beef
Cooked rabbit
Cooked chicken
Cooked lamb
Raw or cooked heart
Little raw liver
Cooked plaice, cod, hake, rock salmon, whiting, haddock, all without bones
Tinned pilchards, sardines, salmon. Little tinned herrings (these are very rich)
Tinned cat foods
Some cooked vegetables such as peas, carrots, etc. may be added
No cooked bones but some cats like a large raw beef bone to chew

5

GROOMING

I SUPPOSE the greatest difference in the care required by the Persian cats as compared with the short-haired cats is in the grooming. Indeed, when it comes to a choice as to which to have, many people, although perhaps preferring a Persian kitten, choose a short-haired, having heard so much about hours spent in looking after a kitten with a long fluffy coat. Others have been told tales about the trouble caused by 'furball' through the swallowing of loose hairs, and think twice about having a Persian.

Having had both long-haired and short-haired cats, I agree entirely that those with the long coats do need more attention than say Siamese, but the time required to be spent on them is usually exaggerated. What is essential is daily grooming, and any one who is willing to spend about fifteen minutes each day on this need have no qualms about choosing a Persian kitten. With daily attention and access to grass either grown in a pot or in the garden, there should be no trouble from 'furball'.

When the kitten arrives at his new home at the age of about ten to twelve weeks, he should be used to being groomed from the age of three weeks and this must be continued. I find a small brush with hair bristles is the best, as many other type of bristle may be too harsh and tear the coat out. I use two combs—one a steel wide-toothed comb set in a metal strip, with a wooden handle, about twelve teeth to the inch, and the other for occasional use for getting dust, fleas and dirt out of the coat is a Spratts No. 6 steel toothcomb.

To start the toilet, a good quality talcum or baby powder should be sprinkled into the roots of the fur. This when brushed and combed completely out will dry-clean the coat, removing dirt and slight grease. Brush the powder thoroughly into the coat, then comb right through several times. Brush again, finishing the coat

46

towards the head so that the long hair or frill stands up all around the face. Finish by gently blowing the fur to make sure that all the powder has gone. This will also help to make the coat stand out away from the body. It is possible to groom to such a point of perfection that each hair stands out separately like thistledown. This effect can only be achieved with practice and patience. Some breeders, although thoroughly experienced in showing, never seem able to achieve this, while others are renowned for the grooming and 'chocolate box' appearance of their cats. It is almost an art to do this and, of course, a great deal depends on the co-operation of the cat. Some love the grooming and all the attention they get and rush in to be brushed when they see preparation for their toilet being made, while others hate it and promptly vanish.

Gentleness is essential. Harsh grooming is painful to the cat and will also spoil the coat by pulling out the fine hair, particularly in the frill around the head, spoiling the appearance.

The very bad dark or grease marks caused along the back by constant stroking may be removed by a gentle rubbing with a piece of cotton wool slightly moistened with methylated or surgical spirits. The fur should be rubbed dry with a piece of rough towelling, the cat being kept away from the fire or a flame in the meantime. It will be dry in a few minutes and the coat may be powdered and brushed in the usual way.

All cats moult, the old hairs gradually loosening and falling out. The late winter and early spring is a particularly bad time for the Persians. If the grooming then is neglected for only a few days, knots and tangles begin to form and the underneath coat soon becomes a mess. If this happens the knots and tangles should be gently teased out with the fingers or with a not-too pointed knitting needle. It may be necessary to cut any very bad matting with a pair of scissors but this should be only done as a last resource and great care must be taken to avoid cutting the cat. The hair will grow again but the cat may not be exhibited with a cut coat, and even if not to be shown it may be many months before the coat looks really beautiful again. If there are any tangles in the coat, groom the cat very gently as these will pull the skin, and this will certainly make the animal bad-tempered and come to dislike grooming. Cats living in the country, as mine do, always seem to pick up prickles, burrs and pieces of bracken, and I go all over them before I attempt to start brushing, picking out anything that has stuck to the fur.

The tail will need special attention. The hair on it must be trained to fan out on each side of the tail so that it is flowing like a plume and in time should be almost the same width as the back. Males' tails, in particular, get yellow stains and scurf near the base and may require gentle washing in a jug of warm lather made from Lux soap flakes. The tail should be rinsed several times, carefully dried and then combed, brushed and powdered.

The ears must be examined daily to make sure there are no signs of canker. Any dust which has collected inside may be wiped away carefully with a little cotton wool but the ears must never be poked inside with a sharp object. If a cat keeps scratching the ear, shaking the head, and the ear appears inflamed, a veterinary surgeon should be consulted as to the correct treatment required.

Persian cats may get dirt in the corners of their eyes sometimes, with even a dark brown matter collecting. This is due to the type and the shortness of the nose. The matter should be gently removed with a little cotton wool and the corners of the eyes wiped. Some cats, perhaps a little over-typed, are inclined to have a 'weepy' eye, and it is essential that this is wiped daily to prevent any blockage. If the weepiness is very troublesome bathing the eye with dampened cotton wool may help, but be careful not to bathe too liberally, allowing water to get up the nose, as the cat will certainly dislike this, and you may do more harm than good as the water may get down into the lungs.

It is the swallowing of the loose hair when washing and licking the coat that may cause furball. A cat is a naturally clean animal and spends hours in grooming, and if brushed and combed daily, given a weekly dose of paraffin, and grass to chew, the small amount of hair then licked down passes through without trouble, and there is no necessity for any long-haired cat to have a fur ball.

To bath or not to bath is a question I am often asked. Personally I have never bathed any of my Blue Persians and have been congratulated at the shows on the condition and the grooming of the cats. I do agree that it might be necessary with the Whites and have gone into the question of bathing in the section on long-haired Whites. I am afraid I cannot agree with one Blue Persian owner I met recently who told me she considered it necessary to bath her cat every week.

6

THE BREEDING QUEEN

IF ONE has a genuine love for cats, the time to give them the care, attention and grooming they need, to have one or two breeding queens is worth-while and rewarding, but not necessarily financially so, the cats and kittens giving many hours of amusement, companionship and affection.

If you do decide to go in for breeding do some serious thinking beforehand, read as much as you can about it, visit cat shows and consult breeders or write to secretaries of cat clubs for advice. Many people buy the first female kitten they see, then when she starts calling decide she might as well be mated and send her to the nearest stud. She will probably produce charming kittens but the owner is frequently disappointed when it is only too obvious that they are not future champions. Buy the kitten which seems to be nearest to the Standard of Points, is lively, happy and healthy, which has a good pedigree, and whose breeder has a reputation for selling first-class breeding stock.

Persians rarely call, or in other words come into season, as early as Siamese and other similar varieties. The earliest, and this is unusual, was a queen I had who called at five and a half months. Cats vary so considerably that although I have tried to find a set pattern, there is none. One will call at seven months for the first time, another at nine, and yet another at twelve months. Some call for about four to five days, others go on for weeks. The period between calls also varies from about three weeks, six weeks, three months, and even six months. The breeding season is usually between February and early October. Do please note that I say usually. Cats are such individualists and so unpredictable that they just do not keep to any set routine. I have had queens call on Christmas Day and they have been mated and produced kittens, but I have found that many queens mated in January, their first call of the season, do not always take and have had to come back again to the stud.

Some Persians are very quiet with their calling and apart from showing even more affection than usual to their owners, and an occasional roll, and a tiny mew or two, give no other signs of being ready for mating, while others can be as noisy as any Siamese, yowling like souls in torment and thumping away with their back legs on the ground until their owner in desperation rushes them away to the nearest suitable stud. From all this it will be realised that a female cat needs guarding well, especially if she tends to be precocious, as it is a great pity to find out that she has found her own mate when she produces a mongrel litter. Not that this will spoil her for any future pedigree mating or have any effect upon any kittens she may produce by later matings. The only harm that may be done is that she may have taken a particular fancy to her first love and will always be endeavouring to get out to meet him again.

When it comes to choosing a stud for the queen try to see him beforehand, choosing one with a good pedigree whose points may correct any bad faults in your female, and you may produce outstanding kittens. I say may, as it is not always so, but you do stand a good chance. Until you have had some experience of breeding avoid using a stud whose pedigree is near to that of your female. Line breeding, i.e. mating mother to son, father to daughter, and sister to brother, used with foresight and knowledge can breed champions, but there is always the hazard that the bad points will be duplicated rather than the good ones.

Stud advertisements appear in *Fur and Feather* and Club Secretaries will often advise and help you to find a suitable male. Once you have chosen one and seen him, if possible, book an approximate time when you think your female will be calling. As I have said before it is not possible to state definitely when this will be. Never send her on the first call, she will probably be far too young, and even if old enough cats are so capricious, the journey may put her off. I consider ten to eleven months is the earliest a Persian should be mated and only then if she appears to be in first-class condition and fully developed. It is unfair to mate a small undersized female and there may be trouble when kittening.

I like the queen to be sent to my stud on the second day, the mating taking place on the third day, but when your female starts to call inform the stud owner with whom you have already been in touch and finalize the arrangements for sending her, either if possible taking the cat yourself or putting her on a train for collection at the nearest station. NEVER send a female unless you are perfectly sure the stud owner is expecting her and prepared to meet her. The stud fee is payable in advance. If by chance she does not take, at the stud owner's discretion a second visit may be made but the expenses incurred must be paid. The basket or box used must be of adequate size allowing her room to stand up and turn around. Don't go to the other extreme and send her in a huge box. She will roll all over the place during travelling, possibly bruising herself and the stud owner certainly won't thank you. I speak from experience having several times been faced with a box more the size of a trunk to get home without aid. There should be a warm blanket inside during cold weather and if a basket is used, brown paper should be tied on around the outside to prevent draughts. The box must be clearly marked 'Live Cat With Care. To be called for'. Guard her well on her return. She may still be in season and will continue to call for a few days more, even a week, and can still be mated if she hasn't taken with the chosen stud and may even have a dual mating.

She is not an invalid but is probably a happy, healthy cat to whom having kittens will be quite a normal procedure, so use your commonsense and do not fuss her. Give her a good mixed diet, plenty of sunshine, freedom and exercise during pregnancy. Increase the food slightly about the fourth to fifth week, if she needs it, but avoid anything too rich. I give my queens Milk of Magnesia in the milk to prevent any acidity when feeding the kittens as this is one of the causes of kittens dying. To help kittening during the last week or two, I put a few drops of olive oil with the food, and on the nipples, after washing, to soften and prepare them for feeding.

The period of gestation is about 63 to 65 days but this may vary by a day or two so there is no cause for panic if the cat eats well and seems perfectly happy but the kittens are a few days overdue. They will probably arrive without any trouble in due course.

GESTATION CHART

Served January.	Due March.	Served February.	Due April.	Served March.	Due May.	Served April.	Due June.	Served May.	Due July.	Served June.	Due August.	Served July.	Due September.	Served August.	Due October.	Served September.	Due November.	Served October.	Due December.	Served November.	Due January.	Served December.	Due February.
1	5	1	5	1	3	1	3	1	3	1	3	1	2	1	3	1	3	1	3	1	3	1	2
2	6	2	6	2	4	2	4	2	4	2	4	2	3	2	4	2	4	2	4	2	4	2	3
3	7	3	7	3	5	3	5	3	5	3	5	3	4	3	5	3	5	3	5	3	5	3	4
4	8	4	8	4	6	4	6	4	6	4	6	4	5	4	6	4	6	4	6	4	6	4	5
5	9	5	9	5	7	5	7	5	7	5	7	5	6	5	7	5	7	5	7	5	7	5	6
6	10	6	10	6	8	6	8	6	8	6	8	6	7	6	8	6	8	6	8	6	8	6	7
7	11	7	11	7	9	7	9	7	9	7	9	7	8	7	9	7	9	7	9	7	9	7	8
8	12	8	12	8	10	8	10	8	10	8	10	8	9	8	10	8	10	8	10	8	10	8	9
9	13	9	13	9	11	9	11	9	11	9	11	9	10	9	11	9	11	9	11	9	11	9	10
10	14	10	14	10	12	10	12	10	12	10	12	10	11	10	12	10	12	10	12	10	12	10	11
11	15	11	15	11	13	11	13	11	13	11	13	11	12	11	13	11	13	11	13	11	13	11	12
12	16	12	16	12	14	12	14	12	14	12	14	12	13	12	14	12	14	12	14	12	14	12	13
13	17	13	17	13	15	13	15	13	15	13	15	13	14	13	15	13	15	13	15	13	15	13	14
14	18	14	18	14	16	14	16	14	16	14	16	14	15	14	16	14	16	14	16	14	16	14	15
15	19	15	19	15	17	15	17	15	17	15	17	15	16	15	17	15	17	15	17	15	17	15	16
16	20	16	20	16	18	16	18	16	18	16	18	16	17	16	18	16	18	16	18	16	18	16	17
17	21	17	21	17	19	17	19	17	19	17	19	17	18	17	19	17	19	17	19	17	19	17	18
18	22	18	22	18	20	18	20	18	20	18	20	18	19	18	20	18	20	18	20	18	20	18	19
19	23	19	23	19	21	19	21	19	21	19	21	19	20	19	21	19	21	19	21	19	21	19	20
20	24	20	24	20	22	20	22	20	22	20	22	20	21	20	22	20	22	20	22	20	22	20	21
21	25	21	25	21	23	21	23	21	23	21	23	21	22	21	23	21	23	21	23	21	23	21	22
22	26	22	26	22	24	22	24	22	24	22	24	22	23	22	24	22	24	22	24	22	24	22	23
23	27	23	27	23	25	23	25	23	25	23	25	23	24	23	25	23	25	23	25	23	25	23	24
24	28	24	28	24	26	24	26	24	26	24	26	24	25	24	26	24	26	24	26	24	26	24	25
25	29	25	29	25	27	25	27	25	27	25	27	25	26	25	27	25	27	25	27	25	27	25	26
26	30	26	30	26	28	26	28	26	28	26	28	26	27	26	28	26	28	26	28	26	28	26	27
27	31	27	MAY 1	27	29	27	29	27	29	27	29	27	28	27	29	27	29	27	29	27	29	27	28
28	APRIL 1	28	2	28	30	28	30	28	30	28	30	28	29	28	30	28	30	28	30	28	30	28	MAR. 1
29	2	29	3	29	31	29	JULY 1	29	31	29	31	29	30	29	31	29	DEC. 1	29	31	29	31	29	2
30	3			30	JUNE 1	30	2	30	AUG. 1	30	SEP. 1	30	OCT. 1	30	NOV. 1	30	2	30	JAN. 1	30	FEB. 1	30	3
31	4			31	2			31	2			31	2	31	2			31	2			31	4

The mother-to-be should be provided with a low flat box sometime before the kittens are due, although she will have to be watched as she may have her own ideas as to where she wants her nursery. Put plenty of clean newspaper in the box, which should be big enough for the cat to lay stretched out in, giving plenty of room for the birth of the kittens. It must not be too high, so that when the kittens are in it she can see in and jump in with no fear of landing on her babies. My cats usually spend many hours a week or two beforehand, tearing up the paper into small shreds, almost making a nest, purring happily all the time. The box should be put in a darkish corner free from draughts. Mine always have their box in the bottom of the airing cupboard in the kitchen. They all realize it is the maternity ward and only go there when expectant, strangely enough ignoring it at other times. Most births are normal, the cat being able to produce, break the cord and wash the kittens herself, but if she has been straining for some time without results or is evidently in distress, the vet should be called without delay. I have managed to ease kittens out with the help of liquid paraffin or Vaseline but great care must be taken.

When all the kittens have arrived the cat should be given a drink of warm milk (I add glucose), the dirty paper removed, and a thick, not thin, blanket folded to the size of the box put in. It is important not to use anything too thin as this may ruck up hiding the kittens and the mother may sit on them. Replace the cat and kittens gently. They will soon be padding away at her sides, even fighting to get at the chosen nipple at that early age. I endeavour to sex them on the second day. The fur grows so quickly in Persians that it soon makes sexing a very difficult problem but do not worry too much. You cannot do anything about it and, very different to mongrel kittens, the females sell just as well as the males.

Sometimes a kitten may seem to be born dead but I have revived several kittens in this way: Make sure the sac or the skin is not still over the face, wipe the mucus from the nose and mouth. Dry all over very quickly with a rough towel as the mother would with her tongue. Place on a well-covered hot water bottle. If there is still no movement, move the front paws very gently up and down, breathing right into the mouth with your mouth. In all probability the kitten will start to open its mouth and breathe normally. Keep warm in an even temperature and when the mother has finished kittening, if it seems to be quite normal and lively, put to the mother for constant warmth and milk.

The queen may surprise you by calling again when her kittens are only a few weeks old. She should not be mated then, but allowed to wean the kittens and get back into first-class condition again before being sent back to stud. Many breeders only allow their Persian Cats to breed once a year but I think it depends on how early in the year the first litter is, as I do not like to have kittens too late in the year for the second litter.

7

THE LITTER

FOR THE FIRST two or three weeks the kittens need little attention, the mother providing food and warmth and washing them. They are usually very quiet and if there is a continuous shrill crying from one, it may be the smallest one not getting his fair share and the others should be taken away while he has a tuck-in. A supplementary feed of an eggspoonful of Lactol or one of the baby foods may help him, given very slowly. I find that even the tiniest kitten will drink from an egg or coffee spoon and will get it more slowly than from a dropper without resultant digestive troubles. I put a drop or two of Milk of Magnesia in the mixture.

The Persians' eyes are usually later in opening than many of the short-haired varieties, ten to twelve days being the usual. Keep the kittens sheltered from strong light until the eyes are well open. If there is any sign of a discharge, swollen eyelids or the eyes are very late in opening, try putting very gently a little Vaseline on the lids and bathing with dampened cotton wool. Take great care in doing this as the water may go up the kitten's nose and cause him to choke. Never pull the eyelids apart as permanent damage may be done this way. Consult a vet if eyelids are still swollen. Sleep, warmth and mother's milk is sufficient for the first week or two. Provide a sanitary tray at the age of three weeks, not too high. Kittens are naturally clean little creatures, almost training themselves given the opportunity. Change the tray frequently. Sand, peat moss, one of the several cat litters now on the market, ashes, earth, even torn up paper may be used. I stand the sanitary tins on large sheets of newspaper as some kittens think it great fun to scatter the litter in all directions.

At three weeks the kittens should be running around their box and climbing out. They will start to play with one another and their mother. They show interest in small balls and will yell when they realize that you are bringing food for them. They will be full of life one minute, and the next asleep in a picturesque group.

I suppose over the years I have had several hundred litters but still to me each litter produces kittens with varying characters and different degrees of intelligence, but one and all without fail are terrible and delightful time-wasters. Whatever variety the first long-haired litter you may breed it may still be not quite what you expected. The Blacks are not black but rusty. The light Self-coloured varieties, as the Blues, have tabby markings, the Chinchillas are quite dark, the Tortoiseshells too show little signs of the beautiful patchings to come but, in a few weeks as the coats grow, their true beauty will begin to appear and you will soon become an expert, or think you are, at picking out the best of the litter.

At the age of three weeks, I start weaning. If there are only one or two kittens, it may be left for another week. To begin with I mix Lactol or one of the well-known baby foods, as for a tiny baby, adding a little glucose. A drop or two is sufficient for the first day. I put a drop on the mouth just to let the kitten get the taste. Some kittens put their little pink tongues out and lick eagerly, but from the expressions I have seen on the faces of others you would think they were being given poison. After a few days, most obviously enjoy the taste and will lick the eggspoonful I give them but I have had a kitten before now positively refuse, even spitting out the milk like a stubborn baby. Unless the kitten appears thin and not to be doing well I do not worry too much. Obviously he is getting enough from his mother and, in time he too will also look for his extra food. I increase the supplementary feeds to two a day and the amount until at the age of about five weeks, the kittens are having a dessertspoonful with Scotts Baby Cereal or Farex added. I give a little cooked minced rabbit, raw scraped beef, or a little cooked boned plaice at this age. By eight weeks they should be on a mixed diet and weaned from their mother, having four small mixed meals a day.

DIET

3–4 weeks   1 egg or coffee spoonful Lactol or Baby Food once a day with added Milk of Magnesia.

| 4–5 weeks | 2 teaspoonsful Lactol or Baby Food with Milk of Magnesia 2–3 times a day. Give in a tiny saucer and encourage to lap properly. |
| 5–6 weeks | Four small meals a day—from scraped raw beef, minced rabbit, chicken, cooked white fish or strained baby foods. Milky feeds as before. |

For further feeding details see General Care.

Even young kittens like drinking water. Remember to have a small bowl only down and change the water regularly. Do not put a large bowl down as water seems to fascinate kittens— they fall in or may, as mine do, smack it with their paws watching the splashes go all over the floor with obvious enjoyment.

A kitten should not be sold before ten to twelve weeks but about eight weeks is the time to start thinking about it. If you are a beginner it is not always easy to sell the first litter but try advertising in the local papers, on notice boards in local shops, telling friends or advertising in *Fur and Feather*. It is very much more expensive I know, but advertising in one of the National evening newspapers may help. Showing helps to become known and therefore also helps to sell.

Before selling, find out as much as you can about the home to which the kitten will be going. Unless you know the person well it is not advisable to sell a whole litter if asked to do so. Beginners may be taken advantage of, the buyer re-selling abroad at inflated prices or there are supposed to be instances of the kittens going for experimental medical purposes.

If you intend to or hope to breed a number of kittens it is in your own interest for you to register for a small fee with the Governing Council of the Cat Fancy, a cattery prefix. This may be one or two distinguishing names or words, mine for instance is Bluestar, and this name is used before each registered kitten's individual name so that it is known at a glance which breeder's kitten it is. This name appears on the pedigree which you supply with each kitten you sell and if the kitten is registered with the G.C.C.F., on the registration form. Any kitten so registered must be transferred from the breeder to the new owner on a special form. Do try and sell your first kittens. I know it is an awful temptation to keep them. It is not so bad selling the first one or two. It is always the last that one hates going but that I am afraid is one of the penalties of being a cat breeder: sadness when the last kitten is sold, but there is always the pleasure of remembering their funny little antics and looking forward to the next litter.

8

THE MALE CAT

UNLESS you intend to go in for breeding seriously and will have three to four females, it is not practicable to have your own stud. To have an unrelated male and female and let nature take its course may seem the obvious thing to do to anyone wishing to start breeding kittens, but it doesn't always work out like that. The male and female may develop and reach maturity at different ages, the male constantly worrying the female or the female yelling her head off and the male wondering what on earth it is all about. Sometimes, too, when a male and female live together all the time, the male will completely ignore her when she is calling. I feel that owners having only one or two queens are well advised to send the queens away for stud rather than having a male as well.

If you decidè to have a stud, visit various breeders, see kittens at cat shows, study the pedigrees well, and judges are sometimes only too pleased to give their opinion on particular kittens, before you finally decide on a male kitten. It should be your aim to get one as near as possible to the standard of points, which should sire kittens that will be a credit to you. If he has done a lot of winning the price asked will be high. Remember it is improbable that you will be able to have him in the house when an adult as a pet, although I had one stud who had perfect house manners all his life. The male cat has an unfortunate, but healthy habit of spraying on literally anything he fancies, making the whole place reek of 'tom cats', so if you do buy a male kitten who will eventually be your stud, do remember he will need a house of his own and a large run on reaching maturity. Don't fuss him too much when a kitten and then leave him alone in his house when grown up. Once he is a proved stud, and the first mating should be with an older queen, rather than with a young cat, he will need two or three females to mate, so for your cat's sake there will have to be visiting queens to keep him happy. The house must be large enough for you to stand up in to supervise matings, and also have enough room to provide separate wired-off accommodation for the visiting queen. There must also be a large window for the stud to see out. My male is fortunate in that we have plenty of woodland for him to roam in, and he is only in his house, with its large run, at night and when he has a visitor. Inside the house is a separate compartment with a small wire run for the female. The stud is able to hold conversations and to get to know her before they actually meet and when I feel she is friendly I allow them to meet. I never leave them alone as some females are vicious after mating, although the male is usually wise enough to spring away from her on to a high shelf provided for that purpose.

Stud work entails considerable work and enormous patience. There are temperamental queens, queens that need coaxing and occasionally easy queens, so that owning a stud and taking visiting queens certainly doesn't mean easy money.

If the queen does not take on her first visit, a second visit may be given for the same fee at the stud owner's discretion, with expenses only being payable for food, etc.

My stud has a thick coat and is very sturdy. He has no heating of any kind in his house and unless the weather is really freezing, the window to his run is always open. I provide a large wooden box and inside this there is a cardboard box filled with shavings and newspaper with a warm woollen blanket on top to make a comfortable bed. I prefer a cardboard box rather than a basket as it is draught-free and can be replaced from time to time.

If a stud has to live in his house and run all the time, he should be allowed exercise in the garden under supervision, if it is at all possible, and allowed to wander at will. Studs are usually the friendliest of animals, loving attention. From their houses they should be able to see everything that is going on and should be spoken to and made a fuss of as often as possible.

His diet must be good if he is expected to sire strong healthy kittens. Mine has the same food as the queens but more of it, with plenty of raw meat, cooked rabbit, liver, and so on. He has plenty of goats milk to drink and clean drinking water is always down. Do watch in the very cold weather that the water is not frozen.

Only accept queens that have been inoculated against Infectious

Feline Enteritis and inspect them well for vermin and skin diseases before placing in the stud's house. Clean the house well with a non-toxic disinfectant after the visitor has gone. He should never be overworked.

9

NEUTERS AND SPAYED FEMALES

IF BUYING a kitten just as a pet do please have the animal neutered as soon as it has developed sufficiently and do not keep putting the operation off saying you will have it done later. It is much more serious when the animal is older.

A male kitten should be ready for neutering when about three months but a veterinary surgeon will advise as to when he considers the kitten has sufficiently developed. The law specifies that an anaesthetic must be given to a cat for any operation, so no food should be given for at least twelve hours before neutering.

The kitten should suffer no ill-effects from the neutering or 'castrating' as it called, and in a very little time will be running around as full of life as ever.

A 'full' male, that is one that is not neutered, can be most unpleasant to have living in the home. Once he becomes an adult his habit of spraying on the wall, furniture and carpet and so on will fill the house with an unpleasant smell, and although in time I am afraid some breeders become used to it, visitors to the household are always rather taken aback. An unneutered tom kept as a pet, and not as a stud, frequently becomes involved in fights over females and may stay away for days, returning home with battered ears and torn fur. A neutered male is the friendliest and the most lovable of all animals, liking his home, and given plenty of exercise and the right kind of food, keeping a good figure and remaining kittenish to the end of his days.

It is unfair to have a female cat as a pet without having her neutered or 'spayed' as it is called. She will come into season frequently attracting all the tom cats around. There is always the possibility too of having mongrel kittens, for which you will have to find homes. There is always a slight danger with anaesthetics being given to cats but modern cat surgery has advanced so far these days that neutering a female is now by no means the big operation it was once considered. The scar involved is now very small and with good post-operative nursing the cat should be herself again in three or four days, with no ill-effects, and there will certainly not be a constant procession of hopeful tom-cats yowling around the house.

Some I know are very much against the neutering of both males and females saying the operation is 'againts nature', but unless one intends to have several cats and to go in for kittens it is surely against nature to keep either a female or a male with no intention of breeding.

10

THE CHARACTER OF PERSIANS

THE PERSIAN is the aristocrat of the cat world. With his long flowing silk coat and the proud expression he looks as if he should spend his life on a velvet cushion with his food being brought to him on siver salvers but, even though he is so decorative, he is as full of fun and mischief as any short-haired mongrel.

If you buy a Persian kitten do not be taken in by his innocent big-eyed gaze. Like all Persians he will sit around in the most photographic poses, like a kitten out of a picture book, then like an uncoiled spring he will pounce on whatever he is pretending is a mouse, that day. He will rush from one room to another like a small tornado, then just as suddenly, he will jump on your lap, settle himself and be asleep in a few seconds, and you will sit there not having the heart to disturb him. You dare not move for he will mutter quietly to himself as, after all, he considers that you are only there for pleasure.

The Persians are very much individualists. They become very attached to their owners but I find they are not dependent on other cats for company. In fact, they seem to revel in undivided attention. While all mine live together in quite happy companionship, I have never found them quite as clannish as the Siamese.

They are talkative, some more than others, with a variety of 'mews' meaning different things. In time one comes to know exactly what each mew means. A 'let me in' mew, a 'don't bother me' mew and a 'thank you' mew all have very different sounds. One has only to sit and watch and listen to a mother with her kittens to realize that their vocabulary is comparitively large. Scolding, grumbling, praising mews all enter into the conversation. Purring is a sign of pleasure but how it is done has not yet been agreed upon. I find cats have different sounding purrs of varying notes, some being a slow steady quiet purr, others loud and almost imperative, while a cat I have now has a break in the middle of hers rather like a faltering car engine. However it is done, it seems to be involuntary on the part of the cat.

The Persians are usually good faithful mothers, showing a great deal of patience with the kittens, loving, fondling and playing with them for hours. They rarely go far from them and I find with mine that if they do leave them, one of the other females usually takes charge.

As in humans, the intelligence varies considerably. Some learn to tap on the window to come in, some stand on their hind legs and rattle door handles to be let in, while others just sit and look and never learn to do anything about it.

I find cats brought up from kittenhood in identical surroundings vary in their nature considerably. Some will always be exceptionally friendly while others are exceedingly nervous, suspicious of strangers and will run and hide on their approach. They are apprehensive of anything unfamiliar and will often advance stiff-legged with ears back and eyes wide-open, but once the object has been sniffed at and found to be harmless no more notice is taken of it.

They have far more expressions than dogs, showing their emotions quite clearly, ranging from pleasure to dislike.

Many people think that the Persians are not good hunters but this has been far from my experience. I have been presented with rabbits, mice, rats, voles, shrews, worms, newts, lizards, snakes and even a stoat, but I am pleased to say very few birds. They watch them and chatter their teeth at them but fortunately very rarely catch one. I never put out food for the birds near the house as I feel it is unfair.

Affection is shown wholeheartedly, paws being put around the neck with a gentle licking of the tongue on the face. They love admiration, both of themselves and their kittens, but are often jealous of extra attention shown to the other cats, sometimes sulking and ignoring me for some time afterwards if they feel they have been left out. They dislike scolding and being shouted at, flicking their tails in digust.

They love playing games and being played with, even the very old cats playing like kittens, hiding toy mice under the carpets and chasing pieces of paper around the room.

They show curiosity about everything but are very adaptable and soon learn to accept changes.

I am often asked for a female kitten in preference to a male, the would-be owner saying they are so much more friendly. I cannot agree with this at all. I have had a number of both sexes as well as neuters over the years and find no difference at all. I felt that a cat will give you as much friendship as you give him and it is your attitude to him that has a great deal to do with his character.

11

SHOWING AND SHOWS

SHOWING and winning at the cat shows is one way of becoming known as a breeder. If one's stock wins consistently, the kittens will be sought after by people in this country and abroad, and the value rises accordingly.

It is not just a question of entering a cat or kitten for a show, taking the animal up, putting it in a pen and waiting hopefully for the judges to give a First Prize card. To begin with, the animal should conform as near as possible to the Standard of Points, type being very important. A cat must be in absolutely first-class condition and not too fat. Preparation must begin many weeks beforehand if the long coat is to be soft, silky and with every hair standing away from the body. Daily attention as in the chapter on grooming is necessary, but care must be taken not to over-groom and pull out the undercoat, particularly around the ruff. Any knots or tangles must be teased out, not cut. This would go against the cat in the judging. The coat must be free from fleas and flea dirts as the vet may disqualify for vermin. The ears must be perfectly clean inside with no signs of canker, the eyes bright and shining with no dirt in the corners or any discharge. Powdering the pale coloured coats should be done daily up to the day before the show, all powder being completely brushed out before judging. The Blacks and Tortoiseshells may be polished with chamois leather, some breeders using a few drops of bay rum. Particular attention must be given to the tail which should be brushed carefully outwards until it is about the same width as the body. Grease stains may be removed with a small piece of cotton wool slightly dampened with methylated spirit, avoiding the eyes if it is anywhere near them. On the night before the show, if powder is used, give a final powdering before grooming as the use is forbidden in the show hall and any cat's coat showing signs of powder may be disqualified.

If the cat is to be bathed, this must be done a few days before the show to allow the natural grease to return to the coat and so that the cat will not catch a chill. See chapter five for bathing.

From the first Show held in this country at the Crystal Palace in 1871, the interest in pedigree cats has been on the increase. Persians were well in the majority in those days, but in a while the Siamese took over, but the number of Persians is increasing again at each show. There are cat shows held all over the country ranging from the largest, the National Cat Club Show held at the Olympia in December, to the cat sections of the various agricultural shows.

The recognized cat shows, that is those held under licence given by the Governing Council of the Cat Fancy, are in three categories, the Championship, Sanction and Exemption. At the Championship shows challenge certificates issued by the G.C.C.F. are given to the winners of the adult open breed classes. A cat winning three of these certificates at three separate Championship shows under three different judges becomes a Champion. There are also Champion of Champion classes with the winner of three champion challenge certificates at three shows under three different judges being entitled to be called a Grand Champion. The Governing Council of the Cat Fancy hold a Supreme Show for cats and kittens that qualify to enter by winning in their open classes at other Championship shows. There is a Best in Show overall winner which is awarded many splendid prizes.

Sanction and Exemption Shows are held under the auspices of the G.C.C.F. but no challenge certificates are awarded.

The last two are usually smaller shows held in all parts of the country. They give the beginner an excellent chance to start showing and to learn the judges' opinions of his cat, and also to see how the animal reacts to being handled and being put in a pen. Some cats really love being shown, preening themselves when admired, while others hide under their blankets just hating it all and resent being handled by the judge and steward.

At shows held under G.C.C.F. all the cats, with the exception of those in litter classes, must be registered at least three weeks before the date of the show, i.e. the details on the pedigree must be entered in the G.C.C.F.'s register and if a cat has changed ownership a transfer certificate must be obtained from the Registrar of the

G.C.C.F., also at least three weeks beforehand. It cannot be shown under the new owner's name unless this has been done. Neuters may be exhibited in special classes only. They may never compete against 'full' cats. Premier certificates are granted to registered neuters winning in their open class. Premierships are given for three separate wins at three shows under three different judges. The cats may then enter the Premier of Premier classes at the shows, and if winning the class at three shows under three judges can become a Grand Premier.

Your cat should be inoculated against Infectious Feline Enteritis at least three weeks before the show. This is not compulsory but when one considers the death rate after cat shows held in the early 1940's when the vaccine was not available and the small amount of deaths in comparison from that devastating disease nowadays, it is only commonsense to have the animal injected well before the show.

The Secretary of the G.C.C.F. will provide a list of cat shows if sent 20p and s.a.e, and then they are advertised in *Fur and Feather*. The Kensington Kitten and Neuter Cat Club hold a Kitten and Neuter Show in July in London. Adult un-neutered cats cannot be shown there. There are a number of Championship shows held in London and the Provinces throughout the year. The later shows are really better for the exhibition of Persians as their coats are usually then at their best.

Show schedules and entry forms giving details of the various classes may be obtained from the Show Manager. One need not belong to a cat club to enter but there are many classes for members only and, if a member of the Club running the show, reduced entry fees. Fill in the entry forms carefully from details on the registration form, quoting the number as any error made may cause disqualification and forfeit of the prize money on checking by the G.C.C.F. Registrar.

A numbered tally with vetting-in card will be sent about a week before the show. This corresponds with the pen number and must be put around the animals neck with white tape. Nothing is allowed in the pen except a warm white blanket and an adequately sized sanitary tin.

Judging begins about 10 when the Hall is cleared. Never

approach your cat or speak to the judge while the judging is in progress. The public are allowed in and the prize cards start to go up about lunch-time when the cat may be fed if necessary. The show closes between 5 and 6 p.m., long distance exhibitors sometimes being allowed to remove their exhibits slightly earlier in order to catch train connections.

Take particular care of your cat on the return home and guard against chills. Keep away from other cats, as even if inoculated, other infection may be brought home. I wipe the coat lightly all over with a mild solution of a non-toxic disinfectant or methylated spirit, give half-teaspoonful of whisky in milk, give a meal of some favoured dish and leave to sleep in a warm room.

12

CARE IN SICKNESS AND CONVALESCENCE

THERE IS an erroneous idea that Persians are delicate, perhaps because some of the wonderful Whites and the Chinchillas have an ethereal look about them. They are normal healthy happy animals, full of energy and playful even in old age. One of my females was a vigorous tree-climber at the age of seventeen. It always saddens me when I hear of cat owners dosing their cats with this and that. I feel that with a correct balanced mixed diet, grass to chew (whether pot-grown or in the garden), clean water to drink, sunshine and plenty of exercise, a cat should be in good condition and no routine dosing necessary. I know cats get worms and need medicine if they are noticed but I do not consider it necessary to worm the cat out every month or so. I feel that doing so is even more debilitating than a worm would be.

A healthy cat is alert and lively. The coat will be silky to the touch and respond to daily grooming. It should not cling lankly to the body, stick out in spikes, or have a rough or staring appearance. The eyes should be bright and wide open, not weepy. The haw or third eyelid should not be up as this is a sign of ill-health or worms sometimes.

If a cat refuses food, seems at all off-colour and sits around moping instead of being his usual cheerful bustling self, I believe in calling in a veterinary surgeon at once. Cats do go down very rapidly and an injection or treatment given quickly may well save the cat's life. A cat may refuse a meal because it is something he does not particularly like, or he may have been out hunting, come home worn out and sleep for hours, but I think any one in close touch with an animal senses when something is wrong. If you suspect your cat is not well, study him carefully, note any particular symptoms and telephone the vet, giving as precise details as you can.

Cats, whether long- or short-haired, suffer from the same major or minor ailments and illnesses but, of course, abscesses and skin diseases such as eczema and ring worm are more difficult to see in the early stages in the Persians, and unless the fur is completely cut off treatment is not easy. Then, on the other side, the long coat does save a cat slightly from minor scratches and bites if involved in a fight.

I give details of some of the ailments which affect cats. There is no reason why your cat should ever suffer from any of them, but if he does, home nursing plays almost as important a part as treatment. Cats are very sensitive to atmosphere, so act normally. Talk to him cheerfully and encouragingly. It may mean day and night nursing, the regular giving of the medicine, and a warm room with a constant temperature. There should be no draughts and the cat must not be allowed to sleep on the cold floor. Strict isolation will be necessary if the illness is contagious. Injections given by the vet will give nourishment during the illness, but when over the worse the appetite may be gone and patience will be needed to make the animal start eating. Never force food down his throat. Brands Essence of Beef or Chicken given in a small teaspoon, warm milk with glucose added, or a little minced rabbit or chicken can be tried. Cats depend on their sense of smell which is often lost during illness. I have found that a few crumbs of fish, pilchards, a little roasted beef, or something with a fairly strong smell will often tempt a convalescing cat. Once he can be persuaded to eat, little and often should be the rule until in a matter of weeks he should be back in condition again.

COMMON AILMENTS AND SERIOUS ILLNESSES

Abscesses

These are fairly common and need careful home treatment. They may be caused by cat fights, scratches, blows or a foreign body causing local infection. A veterinary surgeon may suggest an anti-biotic injection or bathing with hot water, taking care that it is not too hot so as to burn the cat. An abscess is difficult to see in the early stages in the long coats and it is not until the cat sits around looking miserable and cries on being touched or picked up that, on close examination, the painful-looking swelling may be found.

The hair makes treatment difficult. Cut away the fur gently and as close to the skin as possible. Until it comes to a head, the cat may have considerable throbbing pain and there may be a slight rise in temperature. The bathing should be done several times a day until the abscess bursts and the pus runs out freely. It may be lanced once it reaches a head. It is essential that the abscess does not close up too quickly as it may break out again. If possible plug with lint to keep open.

I find once the pus is running freely, the animal is in less pain and seems to appreciate the gentle bathing that is necessary to wash it away. A little hydrogen peroxide poured into the wound will help to cleanse it, or the vet will provide suitable medication for this.

Abscesses are very debilitating and careful nursing and feeding may be necessary to build the cat up to first-class condition again.

A blow on the ear may cause an abscess on the ear flap. The flap becomes filled with serum. This may need lancing and when completely drained the ear flap should be massaged with olive oil to prevent crumpling.

Acidity

Acidity in the mother's milk may be responsible for the death of many young kittens. I have had litters peter out when a week or two old for no apparent reason, the tummies swelling up and the kittens obviously dying in pain. Now I give my queens Milk of Magnesia regularly during prenancy and whilst nursing the kittens. Any kitten showing signs of 'pot-belliedness' is given a drop of Milk of Magnesia. I watch the bowels of any nursing mother with care and give liquid paraffin if at all constipated. There is also a feeling that acidity may cause a queen not to take when mated.

Anaemia

This is a deficiency of red corpuscles in the blood and is fortunately not common in cats. It may be due to a poor diet, too many kittens in too rapid a succession, or can be caused by an injury or be a symptom of severe illness. It may be cured with the correct treatment prescribed by a veterinary surgeon.

Asthma

Generally affects the older cats although it is not a common complaint. As humans, there is a troublesome cough, quick breathing and the attacks are distressing to watch. In between the attacks the cat may not seem all that ill but probably will prefer to stay indoors by the fire. The cat should be kept in an even temperature, have a light diet and be given the drugs advised by the vet.

Bad Breath—*see* Teeth.

Bites

A cat may receive a punctured wound in a fight with another cat. This may turn septic and must be bathed with a mild solution of a non-toxic disinfectant. The hair should be clipped away from the wound and if possible covered with lint to prevent dirt getting in. A bite may cause an abscess.

Bites on the tail are particularly difficult to deal with, needing careful treatment by the vet, with prolonged nursing, as often the wound will refuse to heal and may re-open time and time again.

Bladder Troubles

If your cat strains when passing water or if there is any sign of blood in it, immediate medical treatment is necessary. Very possibly he may have cystitis, or inflammation of the bladder, which can be fatal if neglected. Males kept in runs and neuters who take too little exercise seem to suffer from this condition. Once it has responded to treatment the vet will prescribe tablets to help prevent a recurrence. Slightly sweetened barley water for the cat to drink is a good preventative.

Bronchitis

The symptoms are weeziness, a cough, and trouble in breathing. The cat should be kept in a warm, not hot, even temperature. A vet should be consulted as it may be bronchitis which will respond to early treatment, or the start of a serious infection.

Burns and Scalds

The long coats of the Persians save them from many burns and scalds, although there is the danger of burns from ashes and sparks if a cat will sit too near the fire. The fur will prevent the burning being felt at once. I put a guard in front of the fire before going out and leaving my cats alone in a room. A badly-burnt cat may be in great pain and should be treated for shock. If the burn is a bad one, the fur will not grow on that area again. For mild burns, a covering of white Vaseline will help quick healing. Acid burns should be bathed with a mild solution of bicarbonate of soda.

Canker

This is a general term for various forms of inflammation affecting the ears. The cat may scratch frantically at his ears, shaking the head and holding it down on one side. Until the specific form of inflammation has been diagnosed, it is difficult to treat, as the wrong treatment may worsen the condition and deep poking may harm the ear drum.

Clean inside the ear gently with dampened cotton wool around an orange stick. Wipe away all the discharge and dry well. Canker may be caused by a parasite, a form of eczema, and other infections, and may be exceedingly difficult to cure by home treatment. Nowadays there are various preparations which do clear up the trouble. Your vet will know which is the correct one for that particular inflammation.

I find a wiping of the inside of the ear with cotton wool when grooming will keep the cat's ears clean and canker-free.

A cat living in the country may keep pawing at his ear although there seems to be no signs of canker. There may be a burr, hayseed or some foreign body right inside the ear and this may have to be removed by a vet with forceps. I think the long fur protects the Persians' ears to a considerable extent.

Scratching the ears may be caused by fleas. Several times I have examined my cats' ears to find them lined with minute fleas which they have got from putting their heads down rabbit holes and in hedgehogs' runs. I comb the ears gently with a toothcomb dipped in methylated spirits and rub in a little flea powder advertised as suitable for cats.

Cat Flu or Pneumonitis

Known as cat distemper, cat flu, or more correctly as pneumonitis, this illness affects the respiratory tract with sneezing, running eyes and nose. It has not the fatality rate of F.I.E., but death can be caused through a secondary infection such as bronchial pneumonia. The animal will seem very miserable, may pick at his food or refuse it altogether. Weight will be lost rapidly. The nose is full of mucus and there is a discharge from the eyes. Although as yet there is no vaccine developed that will give complete immunity against this illness, antibiotic treatment if started in the early stages will stop it proving fatal.

Careful nursing in a warm and even temperature is essential, even more so than in other illnesses. The nose and the eyes must be kept mucus-free by bathing gently with cotton-wool dipped in a mild solution of non-toxic antiseptic. The inside of the mouth is often inflamed and this may be gently wiped. I find that most cats appreciate this attention.

Care and feeding as mentioned in the beginning of this section should soon bring the cat back into first-class condition again although, strangely enough, the haw or third eyelid is often left permanently up with no serious results. As cat flu is very infectious, all contacts with other cat owners should be avoided for some weeks after the cat has quite recovered.

Choking

A cat or kitten may choke over too large a lump of meat or a bone may become wedged in the throat and the cat will paw at his mouth in an attempt to dislodge it. Often it will be sicked up and cause no further trouble, but the rounded handle of a small teaspoon used with care will remove the obstacle from the throat, and also a small bone from the roof of the mouth. It is difficult to treat a cat on one's own as it will invariably scratch and bite. I have found that wrapping the animal up as in a cocoon in a thick towel is the best way to handle a cat if alone. If the obstruction cannot be removed, call the vet at once as asphyxia may result.

If a bone has had to be removed, there may be some laceration of the throat, the cat will have difficulty in swallowing and may be

off his food. He should be kept on liquids and soft foods for a day
or two.

Claws

A cat allowed plenty of exercise and freedom should not need the
claws cut. Cutting should never be done by an amateur as claws
tend to splinter badly and the vet will cut them correctly. If there is
no garden with trees for the cat to sharpen his claws, a scratching
block, such as a log of wood, a thick tree branch, or string wound
around the leg of kitchen table, should be provided. A kitten
should be taught when he is young never to sharpen his claws in the
upholstery of the furniture. If scolded each time he attempts to do
this and shown where he may scratch, he will very soon learn to
leave the furniture alone.

Coccidiosis

This is caused by a minute parasite and is known chiefly as
affecting rabbits and baby chicks, but may also affect cats and
kittens through running on ground previously used by these
animals. It causes diarrhoea. Blood may be seen in the motions.
There will be subsequent weakness, and the cat may stop breeding.
It may be necessary to completely disinfect the ground on which
the chickens or rabbits have been running as it can be recurrent
over a long period.

Colds

View any cat or kitten with running eyes and nose, with suspicion.
It may be an ordinary cold or it may be the start of cat influenza or
some other serious illness, so call in your vet. Keep the cat away
from all other cats. If it only turns out to be a cold, nursing as for
humans is most effective. Keep in a warm room, away from
draughts, and give light food only, such as minced cooked rabbit.
Keep the nose and eyes free by wiping with cotton wool dampened
with a mild solution of non-toxic disinfectant. A little Friars
Balsam in a jug of boiling water or a steam kettle in a room will
help to relieve the breathing.

Bronchitis or pneumonia may follow a neglected cold so it
should never be ignored. Care too must be taken that any catarrh

present is soon cleared as it may turn to chronic catarrh or 'snuffles' which affect the Persians with their snub noses in particular. This was once considered practically incurable but drugs may now be prescribed to help clear up the condition.

Constipation
This may be caused by insufficient or incorrect feeding, or lack of exercise. Kittens, going to new homes, frequently suffer from this due to a change of feeding. The diet should be looked into carefully, the food given dampish, and if not included, sardines and a little raw liver may be given. Starchy foods should be cut down and liquid paraffin given for a few days.

Deafness
This is not common but may be found sometimes in the white haired variety with blue eyes. White cats with orange eyes seem to have good hearing. Old cats may be deaf due to wax in the ears and there are also certain diseases of the ear which affect the hearing.

Diarrhoea
Too much cows' milk, a faulty diet or worms may cause diarrhoea. It can also be the symptom of a severe illness and should never be neglected. Fright or a change of diet on coming to a new home may give a kitten an occasional attack but any persistent diarrhoea should receive treatment. Some cats seem unable to tolerate cows' milk at all, and if diarrhoea persists, cows' milk should be withheld. My cats have goats' milk *ad lib* but I should hesitate to say that all cats drink it with impunity, although I do think it is better than cows' milk for them. A little Kaolin powder obtainable from the chemist and mixed with the food may help. Arrowroot or the white of an egg is good. If it persists drugs may have to be administered by a veterinary surgeon. Kittens may suffer from summer diarrhoea through eating fly-infected food and during hot weather or any time really no food or milk should be left around, and the drinking water should be renewed several times a day.

Distemper *see* Cat Flu'.

Dribbling
Old cats frequently dribble through bad teeth or tartar, while I
have had cats and kittens dribble and froth at the mouth when
given medicine or something they did not like. If dribbling badly,
examine teeth and have treated if necessary.

Eczema
A non-contagious skin disease which may be wet or dry. Some
forms are intensely irritating to the cat but others seem not to
affect them at all. It may be inherited or due to bad feeding. Some
cats suffer with it seasonably, particularly in the spring and
summer. In others it may be caused by an allergy. I have seen bad
cases in cats fed exclusively on fish. I had one cat unable to take
cows' milk without the small spots appearing all along her spine. A
change of diet with plenty of variety may effect a cure.

In the Persians it is difficult to see and treat. The hair should be
cut short, and as there are now various preparations which may
bring relief, a vet will prescribe the correct treatment for the type of
eczema involved. In the wet eczema the pus should be bathed
away. If possible the cat should not be allowed to scratch the
affected parts as this will cause sore patches and crusts to form. A
cardboard collar to prevent this can be made quite simply by
making a hole in a circle of cardboard.

Eyes
Normally the eyes of a kitten should open on about the tenth day
without trouble if the mother and her litter are kept in a dim light.
Sometimes kittens are born with their eyes open. If allowed to live
they will probably be blind. If the kittens' eyes do not open and
there appears to be a slight swelling or discharge, bathe with
dampened cotton wool, holding the kitten so that the water does
not run down the back of the nose and choke it. Dry carefully and
smear with a little white Vaseline. If the discharge persists, consult
the veterinary surgeon at once as it may be conjunctivitis which
may destroy the sight even though the eyes are not open.

Cats' eyes are protected by their whiskers and it is rare for them
to get foreign bodies in them, but if they do, bathing gently will
probably wash it away. If the eye is scratched during a fight with

another cat, this too should be bathed frequently. A blow may cause a haze over the eye, or it may be an ulcer needing expert attention. The eyes may be running due to a cold from a draught, or sometimes it is caused by worms. The over-typed Persians do suffer with a brownish discharge from the eyes, which should be bathed away. Never experiment with various eye ointments. They may be all right for humans but not suitable for cats, as it must be remembered that the ointment may contain mercury which is poisonous to cats.

The cat has a third eyelid known as a Haw. It will often be left up after illness and may be regarded as a sign of poor condition. It may sometimes be a sign of worms.

The eyes of the cat are particularly sensitive to light, the pupil reacting to the amount of light, appearing as a narrow slit in daylight and becoming very nearly round in twilight.

Feline Infectious Enteritis

This is the most serious of all cat illnesses but fortunately kittens can be vaccinated with antibiotics very successfully against this terrible virus disease, which previously was responsible for the deaths of thousands of kittens and young cats. The virus is so contagious that a litter may all die within hours of showing the first symptom. It can be carried in clothes, on shoes, by papers and letters, and is also airborne, so an outbreak may start in a district for no apparent reason. If a kitten dies, everything in the house with which the animal has had contact should be destroyed, and the entire premises and all clothes completely disinfected. It is inadvisable to introduce a new kitten into the household for at least six months, and only then if he has been inoculated.

There may be few symptoms, so swift is this disease, and often after death, without a post-mortem, poisoning is suspected. If there is a loss of appetite, listlessness and some vomiting, though this may be slight, call your veterinary surgeon immediately and follow out his instructions precisely. The kitten may seem to shrink before your eyes as dehydration occurs through the lack of white blood cells. The chance of recovery is slight once F.I.E. has been diagnosed, but if the kitten lives for a day that chance exists, and after that careful nursing will be necessary. For the sake of all

other cats or kittens, avoid calling on or writing to any one at all
with a kitten or young cat and handling anybody's cats, for three
months at least, as the virus may still be in your clothes.

Do have all your kittens injected against F.I.E. Consult your vet
as to the correct age and cost.

Feline Infectious Leukaemia (FELV)

Over the years deaths have occurred in cats sometimes for no
apparent reason. Recently it has been realized that some of these
deaths could be due to Feline Infectious Leukaemia, about which
little was known at the time. It can affect cats and kittens in various
ways, including prolonged loss of appetite, fading and so on. It is
now known that it more frequently occurs when a number of cats
live in close contact with one another. A cat brought up entirely
alone, living in the home as the sole pet, is rarely affected.

It is possible to have tests carried out by a veterinary surgeon to
ensure that a cat is free from Feline Infectious Leukaemia.
Research is being carried on at the moment in an endeavour to find
a vaccine for treatment.

Fits

Not so common in cats as in dogs but may effect kittens when
teething or have worms. Years ago I had a Blue Persian kitten that
suddenly dashed around the room, bumping into everything. It
was quite wild and I covered him with a blanket and shut him in a
large cat box. As an amateur breeder I thought the kitten had gone
mad, but the vet came and said that it was all due to teething. After
a sedative and being kept on a light diet for several days, he quite
recovered and never had another fit.

Fleas and Other Parasites

If the cat is constantly scratching and there are no signs of skin
disease, examine carefully for fleas. These are not always easy to
see in the long fur but by blowing aside the hair very small black
specks, like minute pieces of coal, may be seen. These are the flea
dirts, not eggs as often thought, and they indicate the presence of
fleas. Cats do pick up an occasional flea but with the constant
grooming the Persians need, it should be immediately noticed. A

steel toothcomb dipped in methylated spirits should catch the odd one or two, but for a cat to be really plagued with them is very bad indeed. They are most debilitating, may cause anaemia, and can be responsible for worms, as well as making the cat feel quite miserable.

There are a number of preparations on the market advertised as being suitable for cats. Never use one containing D.D.T. as this can be toxic if licked.

Sprinkle the powder well into the roots of the hair, paying particular attention to under the chin, behind the ears and the root of the tail. Put the cat on a sheet of newspaper and stop him from licking himself until the powder has been completely combed out. The fleas will drop on to the paper which should be destroyed at once. Comb with the toothcomb every day repeat the powdering after a week. The fleas do not breed on the cat but are picked up somewhere. They breed in dirt and dust so it is better to try and trace the source of the infection. Make sure the basket and bedding are not harbouring any fleas' eggs or larvae.

Cats living in the country, catching rabbits and rats, get fleas from these creatures so a constant watch is necessary to keep them down.

Lice. Cats may get lice. These are very tiny, grey in colour and may be difficult to see in the fur. Treat as for fleas and repeat for some weeks as the eggs hatch out on the cat and the lice are very hard to eradicate.

Ticks. The small bluish-grey ticks are blood-suckers, clinging most tenaciously by their heads to the skin. Flea powder seems to be useless. Dabbing with surgical spirit is best to make them release their hold. They can be removed with tweezers but there is always the danger that the head may be left in the skin and become a septic sore.

Fractures

Contrary to many beliefs, cats do not always land on their feet after a fall, and some may break limbs after falling from comparatively low heights. Legs may be fractured through road accidents and can be caused through a blow or kick. Any animal with a suspected broken bone should not be moved but should be kept as still as possible. Treat for shock and call in a vet immediately. He may need an X-ray before setting the limb, which will then be put in a splint or a plaster-of-paris bandage. In a young kitten the leg may be tightly bandaged and allowed to heal by itself.

Furball

With daily grooming, especially well during the autumn and spring when the coat is being shed, a weekly dose of liquid paraffin, and grass to chew to act as an emetic, there is no reason why the Persian cats should suffer from fur or hair ball. Usually they sick up an occasional sausage-shaped felt-like mass, but if it becomes too large it may cause the stomach to distend. There will be great discomfort, possibly pain, and if not passed it may necessitate an operation.

Mange

Unlike eczema this is most contagious. There are two kinds, both caused by parasites burrowing under the skin. The common variety affects the head and neck chiefly, the cat scratching constantly, with the hair falling out and bare patches appearing.

Sarcoptic mange or scabies is highly contagious to other cats and humans, with the fur breaking and bare patches spreading along the spine. Follicular mange is not nearly so common and of the two not so easy to treat but can be cured.

Mange is a very nasty compaint in the long haired cats as unfortunately it is not always seen in the early stages when a cure is much easier. The hair should be shaved off. Diagnosis by the vet with a strict adherence to the treament prescribed will bring about a cure in the long run.

Poisons

Cats may be poisoned by eating treated meat put down to destroy vermin, although as they are are fastidious in what they choose to eat, poisoning is not as prevalent as one might think. Fly sprays and flea powders containing D.D.T. have been proved to be toxic to cats and should not be used when the animals are around. Creosote, the deadly poisons such as arsenic and strychnine, chewing grass and treading on paths treated with weed killers have also been found to be responsible for the deaths of some cats.

I have just received a note from the United States saying that the rhododendron, philodendron, the African Violets and/or other plants with woody stems have been proved to poison cats who nibble them. Cat owners are advised to keep them well out of reach.

Copper sulphate is sometimes used to clean out small garden pools. If cats are allowed to drink from these constantly over a period, it may prove fatal in the end.

Consult a veterinary surgeon at once if any type of poisoning is suspected. He will know the correct treatment, as for some poisons it is necessary to give an emetic, while with others it may be wrong to do so.

Rheumatism
This may affect a very old cat, making him move very stiffly. The leg joints may be swollen and the animal dislike being picked up. Drugs may help and keeping warm, away from draughts.

Rickets
This is caused by a calcium deficiency with consequent bone weakness. It is sometimes found in young kittens due to incorrect feeding of the mother and the babies. Cod liver oil or halibut liver oil, with lime water added to the milk feed, fresh air and sunshine should bring a cure.

Ringworm
May be contracted by both humans and cats and can be transmitted from one to another. There are several kinds caused by a fungus. The hair roots are affected and the fungus spreads, making the characteristic round paches. Urgent veterinary treatment is essential, but in the long-haired cats unfortunately it may spread undetected as it is not always seen in the beginning. It was once considered incurable in cats, but fortunately there are now ointments and antibiotics on the market which make a cure possible.

Sickness

Cats are sick fairly frequently after chewing grass. This is natural, helps to bring up loose fur, and is no cause for worry. Sometimes too, if very hungry, a bolted meal will be brought up again, but any persistent vomiting with yellow or white froth should be reported to the veterinary surgeon. It may be just gastric trouble or can also be the start of one or two serious illnesses.

Teeth

As a general rule cats' teeth need very little attention nor do they appear to have toothache often. The twenty-six baby teeth begin to come through about the age of three weeks and although kittens may suffer sore gums, they seem to give very little trouble. Between the age of five and six months, the thirty adult teeth start to appear and here again the majority of kittens cut and lose the milk teeth easily, and the owners may be startled to find an odd tooth or two around the house as they frequently drop out. A few do have fits, suffer from sore gums, and run a slight temperature referred to as a temperature mark, which will cause a bar to appear in the long fur as it grows out. Give a small dose of Milk of Magnesia daily while the teeth are being cut, and a large beef bone to gnaw on.

Cats' teeth are not adapted for crunching bones but act like scissors in eating flesh. Cooked bones which will splinter should never be given but a raw bone may be liked.

Old cats may get an accumulation of tartar on the teeth causing irritation of the gums and the loosening of the teeth. It may be necessary for the vet to remove such tartar and also to pull out any bad or broken teeth. If left, the gums may become inflamed and an abscess may result. If a cat pulls at his mouth with his paws or is given to dribbling, the teeth and gums should be examined for any signs of trouble.

Tranquillizers

These must not be administered to a cat prior to a show. If a cat is so nervous that he cannot be handled without them, he should not be shown. The G.C.C.F. Show Rules now state that a cat may be disqualified if it shows signs of having been given a tranquillizer. It has been found that the effect of the drug may wear off during the show. The cat will then be even worse than if he had never been given the drug and will fight madly when handled.

If a nervous cat has to go on a long journey or a cat is known to be badly affected by travelling, the vet will give or prescribe any tablets he thinks fit.

Worms

A kitten does not have to have worms but if there are any signs he should be wormed. An adult cat may suffer seriously from tape worms and directly these are noticed he will need treatment, but do let your veterinary surgeon give the correct medicine and what is more tell you the correct dosage. Incorrect worming is responsible for many cats' and kittens' deaths.

Tape Worms can be extremely lowering and weakening. They usually affect the young and older cat rather than a kitten. A staring coat, large appetite with no increase in weight, the haws up, weepy eyes and lack of energy may all be symptoms of tape worms. Small white pieces or segments may be seen under the tail or sticking to the coat. There is no need for starvation with the new drugs your vet will prescribe.

Round Worms. Even if round worms are suspected, the kitten should not be given treatment until at least nine weeks old. Round worms are not so troublesome in adults as in young kittens who will probably have little pot bellies, ragged-looking and be-draggled coats, ravenous appetites and running eyes. The small thin white worms may be seen in the motions. Regular dosing for a short period with liquid paraffin may get rid of a slight infestation, but if more serious a vet will prescribe piperazine, which is a safe remedy.

Worms, whether round or tape, can be most lowering and after treatment the cat should be given plenty of good food, sunshine and exercise to regain top condition again.

13

PEDIGREES AND REGISTRATIONS

A PEDIGREE kitten is one whose parents, grandparents and great-grandparents are known, and are of pure stock. To any one interested in breeding, who has a pre-knowledge of the cats mentioned on the pedigree, it can tell a great deal about the type, whether from a prolific strain and if from champion stock. For a pet kitten that is to be neutered the pedigree is important only in that it is an indication that the breeding is known and is pure. Naturally if you wish to go in for breeding, before buying a kitten it would be wise to seek advice from the experts, either by attending a show and talking with the judges or visiting the breeders in their homes. It is better for a beginner not to buy a kitten that is too closely bred. Line breeding should only be carried out if the cats are known. It is always risky mating too closely as inbreeding tends to bring out the bad faults in that particular line, such as kinked tails, inverted eye lids and distorted back legs.

It is not necessary to register kittens but most breeders like to do this particularly if they have a prefix, that is a distinguishing name which is used in front of the kitten's name each time they register a kitten. It is thus possible to know at once who has bred a particular animal. If it is a persistent winner at the shows the breeder's name will soon become well known and the kittens with that prefix will be sought after.

The Governing Council of the Cat Fancy keep a book with all the cat registrations in it. On application to the Registrar a form may be obtained for registering a litter or just one kitten. On filling in the information required, which is much the same as on a pedigree, subject to approval of the chosen name (no duplication is allowed), and on payment of a small fee, a numbered registration certificate will be issued.

Any registered kitten which is sold must be transferred to the new owner on a special tranfer form issued by the G.C.C.F. for a small payment, who also keep a record of all such tranfers. This certifies the change of ownership and if the new owner wishes to show the kitten, the transfer must have taken place at least three weeks before the show. It is possible to register a kitten without a prefix but it may be difficult to find a name that has not already been used.

THE GOVERNING COUNCIL OF THE CAT FANCY

Affiliated Cat Clubs and Cat Societies throughout Great Britain elect delegates annually at a General Meeting or by postal ballot. These delegates representing the various clubs and societies compose the Governing Council of the Cat Fancy and from these the Council elect a Chairman and officers to sit for that year.

The Governing Council approve the dates of shows held under its licence, and provide and pay for Registrars who are responsible for the registering and transferring of cats and kittens.

Its aim is to improve and advise on cat breeding and cat welfare. It classifies cat breeds, approving, recognizing and granting breed numbers to new varieties as the occasion arises, and issuing a booklet giving the approved standard of points of all the recognized breeds. The Council issue an annual list of Cat Shows to be held under its jurisdiction and a list of Cat Clubs with the names and addresses of the secretaries It has the power to censor and suspend cat breeders for any serious violation of the Council's rules and regulations regarding shows, showing and the cat welfare generally.

The Secretary of the Council is Mrs. W. Davies, G.C.C.F., Dovefields, Petworth Road, Witley, Surrey. Send her s.a.e. for address of appropriate Registrar.

THE CAT CLUBS

There are many Cat Clubs and Societies all over the country whose members share a common interest in pedigree cats. Some hold various social functions, and put on shows, and all hold an annual general meeting. It is not necessary to be a breeder to belong to a club, but if considering exhibiting, the various clubs put on classes at a number of other shows, in which their members may enter. I give below the various Clubs that specialize in long-hairs, but as the secretaries do change frequently, it is advisable to write to the Secretary of the Governing Council of the Cat Fancy, Dovefields, Petworth Road, Witley, Surrey (enclosing 20p) for an up-to-date list of the Clubs, with names and addresses.

Blue Persian Cat Society
Black and White Cat Club
Capital Long-Hair Cat Association
Celtic Long-Hair Cat Society
Chinchilla, Silver Tabby & Smoke Cat Society
Colourpoint, Red Coated & A.O.V. Club
Colourpoint Society of Great Britain
East Anglian Persian Cat Society
Kent Long-Haired Cat Club
Long-Haired Cream and Blue-Cream Association
North of Britain Long-Hair Cat Club
The Tabby Cat Club
United Chinchilla Association
White Persian Cat Club
Red, Cream, Tortie, Tortie and White Blue Cream and Brown Tabby Society
Colourpoint Cat Club

There are also a number of All-Breed Clubs that welcome members interested in any variety of cats, such as the National Cat Club.

ANIMAL WELFARE SOCIETIES

As most readers will know, there are throughout the country a number of voluntary animal welfare societies whose concern is for the house cat and stray cats as well as other animals. In most cases the societies will give free advice on the care of cats, issue pamphlets and endeavour to find homes for or destroy unwanted cats and kittens. Some provide veterinary treatment, including neutering and spaying, for those unable to pay or for a contribution. All recommend having both male and female pet cats neutered. I give below the names and addresses of the chief ones. For the nearest branch and any other information required, a stamped addressed envelope should be sent to the secretary at the head office of the society with which you wish to get in touch.

The Cats' Protection League, 7 North Street, Horsham, Sussex. (Deals with cats only.)

Royal Society for the Prevention of Cruelty to Animals, Manor House, The Causeway, Horsham, Sussex.

The Blue Cross Society, 1 High Street, London, S.W.1.

The People's Dispensary for Sick Animals, P.D.S.A. House, South Street, Dorking, Surrey.

14

GENERAL INFORMATION

Cats and the Law

There are a number of laws in this country relating to animals. Cats may not always be specially mentioned but they have the same rights as any other animals. They are protected against unnecessary suffering, being deliberately frightened, tortured, hurt, injured, abandoned or stolen, nor may they be shot for trespass alone. Anyone putting down poison to destroy vermin must make sure that it cannot harm cats. Some poisons advertised as killing rats and mice but as being safe for domestic animals, may poison a cat eventually by accumulation, particularly if he eats rats or mice which have died from that poison. The owner of a cat cannot be prosecuted for any damage a cat may do when following its natural instincts. An anaesthetic must be given to a cat for any vital operation.

Importing and Exporting

Importing. It is not possible to import or bring back a cat or kitten to this country and take it straight to your home. Anyone returning to or entering this country, whether by sea or air, and bringing a cat, must have obtained permission and made arrangements for the animal to go into quarantine for a period of six months. A landing order licence may be obtained from the Ministry of Agriculture, Animal Health Division, Hook Rise, Tolworth, Surrey, who will also supply a list of quarantine catteries. On arrival, as no contact is allowed, the collection and carrying must be done by an approved carrying agent. To prevent the animal suffering too badly from the separation, arrangements should be made for frequent visiting.

Exporting. Outstanding British cats and kittens of all breeds are sought after by many breeders overseas. Naturally, they expect only to receive the best and it is up to the members of the Cat Fancy to see that they get it, as it is an expensive business with the price and the cost of sending. An Import licence is needed by most countries. Whether sent by sea or by air the cat must be in an adequate container. I have had them made of light but substantial plywood by a local carpenter, but one or two of the Air Companies, Spratts and other carrying companies will usually supply them at a reasonable cost. Most countries now require cats and kittens to have received rabies injections before leaving Britain.

Quarantine
No cat may be brought into this country as a precaution against the introduction of rabies, unless the animal goes into quarantine in a recognized kennel or cattery for a period of six months. Arrangements must be made well in advance through the Ministry of Agriculture and Fisheries. Heavy fines or imprisonment, may follow if caught attempting to smuggle a cat or kitten into Britain.

Boarding
One of the snags in having a cat or cats is the holiday period when provision has to be made. It may be necessary to find a boarding cattery. The local animal welfare societies and cat clubs may be able to supply names and addresses. Your veterinary surgeon may be prepared to look after your cat or know someone he can recommend.

There are many boarding establishments and before definitely deciding on one, if possible visit it and see the accommodation offered to make sure that your cat will be comfortable and well looked after. You will probably be asked to bring a vet's certificate giving the animal a clean bill of health and also stating that he has been inoculated against Infectious Feline Enteritis. This is a safeguard for your cat as well as for the other cat boarders.

Travelling
Many cats enjoy travelling around with their owners. The Persians as a whole do not take so readily to being taken around on a lead although I have seen some who were quite happy about it and

looked forward to going for a walk. Others like to go for car rides and will sit looking out of the window with obvious enjoyment, but there are some who positively hate travel in any form, dribble continuously, sit panting or mewing frantically. If your cat dislikes travelling it is far better to put him in an escape-proof basket where after a while he will usually quieten down. I find such cats settle down much quicker in a train than in a car. If sending unaccompanied by railway, provide an adequate sized box or basket, that is one that the cat can stand up in and turn around. The railway staff are usually very good about the comfort of animals and I know of several cases when they have refused to accept (quite rightly) cats that were being sent in too small containers. The basket or box should be labelled in large block capitals with the consigner's name, telephone number and the station at which he is to be met. I always put it twice in case one label becomes mutilated in any way. The railway company will provide a Livestock label. Put your address inside the container not outside.

If a cat is to travel by air, the Air Company concerned will supply details of their requirements as to containers, food, etc. I do not think any kitten should be sent abroad under the age of three months.

By Underground and Bus
The London Transport allow cats to be carried on buses and coaches free of charge at the conductor's discretion. While they may be taken on leads, it is preferred that they are in a basket, and a conductor is not always willing to have several cat baskets on his bus and can, and does sometimes, refuse permission, so if on your way to a cat show allow adequate time for such hitches. On the Underground cats may be carried free of charge but here it is also preferred that they be in baskets. Provincial bus companies, such as the National, may make a small charge for the carrying of a cat in a basket.

INDEX